Lives of Jesus Series

LEANDER E. KECK, *General Editor*

JESUS
ON SOCIAL
INSTITUTIONS

by

SHAILER MATHEWS

Edited and with an Introduction by
KENNETH CAUTHEN

FORTRESS PRESS

Philadelphia

Library of Congress Catalog Card Number 72-139346

2712H70   Printed in U.S.A.   1-156

CONTENTS

* Pagination from this page forward is identical with that of the
original 1928 edition.

FOREWORD
TO THE SERIES

In a time when a premium is placed on experimentation for the future and when theological work itself values "new theology," the reasons for reissuing theological works from the past are not self-evident. Above all, there is broad consensus that the "Lives of Jesus" produced by our forebears failed both as sound history and as viable theology. Why, then, make these works available once more?

First of all, this series does not represent an effort to turn the clock back, to declare these books to be the norm to which we should conform, either in method or in content. Neither critical research nor constructive theology can be repristinated. Nevertheless, root problems in the historical-critical study of Jesus and of theological reflection are perennial. Moreover, advances are generally made by a critical dialogue with the inherited tradition, whether in the historical reconstruction of the life of Jesus or in theology as a whole. Such a dialogue cannot occur, however, if the tradition is allowed to fade into the mists or is available to students only in handbooks which perpetuate the judgments and clichés of the intervening generation. But a major obstacle is the fact that certain pivotal works have never been available to the present generation, for

they were either long out of print or not translated at all. A central aim, then, in republishing
certain "Lives of Jesus" is to encourage a fresh
discovery of and a lively debate with this tradition
so that our own work may be richer and more
precise.

Titles were selected which have proven to be
significant for ongoing issues in Gospel study and
in the theological enterprise as a whole. H. S.
Reimarus inaugurated the truly critical investigation of Jesus and so was an obvious choice. His
On the Intention of Jesus was reissued by the American Theological Library Association in 1962, but
has not really entered the discussion despite the
fact that questions he raised have been opened
again, especially by S. G. F. Brandon's *Jesus and
the Zealots*. Our edition, moreover, includes also
his previously untranslated discussion of the resurrection and part of D. F. Strauss's evaluation of
Reimarus. That Strauss's *Life of Jesus* must be
included was clear from the start. Our edition, using
George Eliot's translation, will take account of
Strauss's shifting views as well. Schleiermacher's
Life of Jesus will be translated, partly because it
is significant for the study of Schleiermacher himself and partly because he is the wellspring of
repeated concern for the inner life of Jesus. One of
the most influential expressions of this motif came
from Wilhelm Herrmann's *The Communion of the
Christian with God,* which, while technically not a
life of Jesus, emphasizes more than any other work
the religious significance of Jesus' inner life. In
fresh form, this emphasis has been rejuvenated in
the current work of Ernst Fuchs and Gerhard

Ebeling who concentrate on Jesus' own faith. Herrmann, then, is a bridge between Schleiermacher and
the present. In such a series, it was also deemed
important to translate Strauss's critique of Schleiermacher, *The Christ of Faith and the Jesus of
History,* for here important critical issues were
exposed. Probably no book was more significant for
twentieth-century study of Jesus than Johannes
Weiss's *Jesus' Proclamation of the Kingdom of
God,* for together with Albert Schweitzer, Weiss
turned the entire course of Jesus-research, and
undermined the foundations of the prevailing
Protestant theology. From the American scene,
two writers from the same faculty were included:
Shailer Mathews's *Jesus on Social Institutions* and
Shirley Jackson Case's *Jesus: A New Biography.*
There can be no substantive dialogue with our own
theological tradition which ignores these influential
figures, though today they are scarcely read at all.
Doubtless other works could have been included
with justification; however, these will suffice to
enliven the theological scene if read perceptively.

    In each case, an editor was invited to provide an
introductory essay and annotations to the text in
order to assist the reader in seeing the book in perspective. The bibliography will aid further research,
though in no case was there an attempt to be comprehensive. The aim is not to produce critical
editions in the technical sense (which would require
a massive apparatus), but a useable series of texts
with guidance at essential points. Within these aims,
the several editors enjoyed considerable latitude in
developing their contributions. The series will
achieve its aim if it facilitates a rediscovery of an

exciting and controversial history and so makes our
own work more fruitful.

In the case of Shailer Mathews, it was decided to
publish *Jesus on Social Institutions* rather than the
book it replaced, *The Social Teachings of Jesus*
(1897). This was not an easy choice, for the earlier
work was by far the more popular and influential.
Nonetheless, since Mathews's views were not static,
it was judged best to introduce him by way of his
more mature conclusions and to take account of the
earlier book in the Introduction and annotations.
Moreover, it is the present volume which contains
the suggestive contention that Jesus must be understood in terms of the psychology of revolution
because he was shaped by Jewish apocalyptic. Since
both the theology of revolution and the rediscovery
of apocalyptic are increasingly important today,
it is appropriate that *Jesus on Social Institutions*
be the book in the series.

The present volume has been prepared by Dr.
Kenneth Cauthen, Professor of Christian Theology
at Colgate-Rochester/Bexley Hall/Crozer, Roches-
ter, New York. A Georgia Baptist, Dr. Cauthen
was educated at Mercer University (B.A., 1950),
Yale Divinity School (B.D., 1953), Emory University (M.A., 1955) and at Vanderbilt (Ph.D., 1959).
Prior to his present position, he was Professor
of Christian Ethics at Mercer University from
1957–61 and Professor of Theology at Crozer Theological Seminary from 1961–70. Though not a
New Testament scholar by trade, he is well equipped
to introduce readers to Shailer Mathews, having
investigated the phenomenon of American religious

liberalism in his doctoral dissertation.[1] Following this Cauthen turned to a consideration of the relationship of science and theology in order to work out a synthesis of evolutionary modes of thought and a Christian understanding of God.[2] At present he is engaged in efforts to correlate theological and secular concern with the future as a way of developing a strategy of hope. He expects this to take the form of "biopolitics," a future-oriented conceptual scheme which takes life and its fulfillment as the central motif of thought and action.[3]

LEANDER E. KECK

[1] Kenneth Cauthen, *The Impact of American Religious Liberalism* (New York: Harper, 1962).

[2] Kenneth Cauthen, *Science, Secularization and God* (New York: Abingdon Press, 1969).

[3] Kenneth Cauthen, "The Case for Christian Biopolitics," *The Christian Century* 86 (1969): 1481–83.

EDITOR'S PREFACE

What a pleasure it has been to turn again to the works of Shailer Mathews a decade after I originally examined his thought with some care for purposes of a graduate thesis. His method and outlook seem more worthy of reconsideration today, due both to the weakening in my own mind of the neoorthodox framework which then guided my evaluation of him and to the changed setting of theological inquiry. In a time when the reality of God and the meaningfulness of God-language are central, his "conceptualist" view of God is worthy of a hearing. When theologies of hope are coming into prominence, the evolutionary, organic perspective within which he viewed the idea of a forward-moving purposeful cosmos is not to be despised. His thesis respecting the way theology interprets the Christian heritage anew each generation by making use of patterns taken from the contemporary social mind holds its own in comparison with Tillich's "method of correlation." Mathews's way of relating the ethical imperatives of Jesus to the apocalyptic framework in which they appear, his conception of what is transient and what is abiding in Jesus' social teachings, and even his conception of the quest of the historical Jesus are not obsolete by any means. In short, Shailer Mathews is not simply a man from the past but in several respects is a contemporary partner in theological dialogue, especially for those interested in forging an American tradition.

The introduction which follows deals with the overall theological perspective of Mathews and not merely with his approach to the life and teachings of Jesus. This reflects my own interests as a theologian. Doubtless, New Testament scholars will wish at points for a more acute awareness of issues related to the study of the life of Jesus and to the particulars of exegesis. Nevertheless, I believe the relevance of Mathews to the larger problems of theological inquiry, today justifies the procedure followed even if this involves neglect of some details of his work as a New Testament historian.

I wish to offer a special word of gratitude to the Ph.D. dissertation of my colleague Kenneth Smith, whose detailed investigation of the work of Shailer Mathews has helped me immensely. I wish to thank also Steve McKnight, my student assistant, for suggestions resulting in improvements in the style and wording of numerous sentences. His wife, Becky, deserves praise for her care in typing a manuscript pretty badly mangled by myself and her husband.

KENNETH CAUTHEN

THE LIFE AND THOUGHT OF SHAILER MATHEWS

Kenneth Cauthen

THE LIBERAL FRAMEWORK OF MATHEWS'S THOUGHT

> What is modernism? That is what Shailer
> Mathews teaches at the University of Chicago.
> What is fundamentalism? That is what Shailer
> Mathews preaches to the Northern Baptist Con-
> vention.

This sequence making the rounds four decades ago
reflects the close connections Shailer Mathews had
with both the practical life of the churches and the
academic study of theology. What is important for
purposes of this introduction is that one cannot
understand the work of Mathews as a teacher and
scholar apart from some grasp of that many-sided
movement in American Protestantism to which the
term modernism or liberalism is generally attached.
In this context, liberalism refers to that school of
thought running its course in this country between
the Civil War and World War II, which sought to
reconcile the ancient gospel with modern culture.[1]

[1] What is called "liberalism" is a multifaceted phenomenon with
diverse roots. The intellectual milieu, as sketched in the following paragraphs, affected Continental Protestant theology ever since D. F.
Schleiermacher's *On Religion: Speeches to its Cultured Despisers*
(1799). In America, however, the liberal effort to reformulate Christian
truth in accord with modern culture began somewhat later (if one disregards the Deist-Unitarian tradition which was pitted against Calvin-
ism), and was not directly influenced by Schleiermacher. For a fuller
account of the nature and history of liberal Protestant theology in
America, see my *The Impact of American Religious Liberalism* (New
York: Harper, 1962).

Harry Emerson Fosdick spoke for all liberals when he wrote that he wanted to be both ''an intelligent modern and a serious Christian.'' [2] The methods, the presuppositions, and the categories of Protestant orthodoxy were thought to be obsolete in the new intellectual, moral, and social situation which had emerged. Liberals differed among themselves with regard to the way in which this accommodation to culture could best be carried out, but they agreed that restating the Christian message in a contemporary idiom was the overriding theological task of the age. In place of liberalism, Mathews preferred the alternative term, modernism, a word that came to be associated with the viewpoint of liberalism's left wing. The modernists' special concern was with method, although they too sought to preserve the abiding truths and values of the historic tradition in a form that was both credible and relevant in today's world.

Before dealing directly with Mathews, then, let us look briefly at some of the background elements— both intellectual and social—which helped to shape modernist thought. The Renaissance and Reformation had unleashed new forces that interacted in a complex way upon the mentality of Western man and that raised new problems for Christian theology. The findings of modern science and the results of the historical-critical study of the Bible, the latter increasingly imported from Germany, undermined orthodox views of the inspiration of Scripture. In particular, science not only demonstrated that the cosmology of the Bible was false but also seemed to

[2] Harry Emerson Fosdick, *The Living of These Days* (New York: Harper, 1956), p. vii.

disclose an orderly world developing in accordance with its own immanent laws in such a way as to rule out or make unnecessary any supernatural intervention in its processes. Moreover, science's successes in uncovering the secrets of nature magnified the value of empirical methods of discovering truth as over against reliance on traditional authority. Critical-historical study of the Scriptures showed that there were disparities and developments in theological perspective within the Bible itself and brought to light the vast differences between the ancient biblical categories and the ideology of the modern world. Studies of the history of Christian thought revealed that the classical theologies of the past were likewise relative to their own time and place. The philosophers of the Enlightenment exalted the rights of reason over against revelation, stressed the inherent goodness and perfectibility of man, and viewed history as an upward march of perpetual progress. Kant gave powerful testimony in favor of a morally-based faith in God within the limits of reason alone and made ethics and religion into autonomous realms, independent of biblical authoritarianism on the one hand, and of scientific materialism and philosophical scepticism on the other. Idealism and romanticism viewed the world as an organic unity pervaded by an Immanent Mind which progressively imparts its divinity to nature, history, and to the human spirit. While the idealists stressed reason and the romanticists exalted intuition, they agreed that Divine Reality is knowable without special revelation. Pietism, expressing itself in America as revivalism, stressed the immediacy and certainty of the knowledge of God given in indi-

vidual religious experience, thus lessening dependence on doctrinal correctness. The Darwinian
theory of organic evolution had a many-sided impact
on the intellectual milieu of the times, contributing
to the emphasis on the immanence of God, the
dynamic character of the world process, the continuity between nature, man, and God, and progress as
the key to the understanding of both cosmic and
human history.[3] Modern democracy with its confidence in man, its egalitarianism, and its individualism worked against theological doctrines based on
divine sovereignty. Democratic theory gave impetus
to the demand that the idea of God be modified to
allow the rights of man to put limits on the preroga-
tives of deity.

All of these influences—and doubtless there were
others also—created a cultural climate which alien-
ated a growing number of theologians from the prevailing Calvinistic orthodoxy and set in motion the
forces which resulted in the emergence of liberalism
as the leading theological perspective in the academic world during the first three decades of the
twentieth century. These factors can be summarized
under three headings: (1) those which emphasized
continuity in the world and between nature, man,
and God, (2) those which stressed the autonomy of
reason and religious experience rather than the
authority of special revelation, and (3) those which
magnified the dynamic and developmental character
of nature, history, and culture. Continuity, autonomy, and dynamism—these were the three funda-

[3] For a brief survey of the impact of Darwin, see Bert James Loewen-
berg, *Darwinism Comes to America 1859–1900*, Facet Books, Historical
Series (American Church), 13 (Philadelphia: Fortress, 1969; reprint
of *The Mississippi Valley Historical Review*, 28 [1941], pp. 339–368).

mental motifs which guided the reconstruction of the Christian message and which led to the emergence of a liberal theology whose basic conceptions were the immanence of God, the priority of reason and/or religious experience, and the evolutionary and progressive nature of the world process. The result was a theology which pointed to a unified, dynamic world indwelt by an Immanent Spirit who can be intuitively (and/or empirically or rationally) known and who is gradually bringing mankind to a more or less perfected state of personal and social existence on earth. When the Bible and the Christian tradition were interpreted within this framework, some form of theological liberalism was born.

Along with the intellectual challenge to orthodoxy went a simultaneous social challenge. Though the relationship between the rise of liberalism and the birth of the Social Gospel is not a simple one, it is clear that the two movements are closely related. On the religious and theological side the Social Gospel inherited the widespread concern in nineteenth-century American Christianity for a righteous society on earth. On the intellectual side the movement drew from a wide variety of philosophical, political, and economic sources of a critical and reformist nature, including Marxian and English socialism, utilitarianism, theories of evolutionary progress, and the views of such men as Herbert Spencer, William Sumner, Lester Ward, Edward Bellamy, Henry George, Leo Tolstoi, Henry Lloyd, and others. The religious and cultural currents combined with the optimism, activism, and pragmatism of America (with its dream of a perfected commonwealth in the new world) to furnish the materials for a fresh interpretation of the relevance of the gospel to an increasingly urban, industrial nation. It was, however, a series of crises in the last quarter of the nineteenth century that was immediately responsible for generating a concern with the structures of society. Strikes, riots, depressions, and unemployment dealt a profound blow to the complacent *laissez-faire* attitudes, characteristic of American Christianity, and made it evident to many that a new social program was badly needed by the churches.

While various theologies were reflected in the response the denominations made to the challenge of the new industrial, urban climate, it was liberal theology that undergirded the developing Social Gospel movement. Washington Gladden, who has been called the father of the Social Gospel, was also a prominent liberal theologian. By 1900 this movement had begun to reach its maturity under the leadership of Gladden, Josiah Strong, Richard Ely, Francis Peabody, and others. Walter Rauschenbusch became the acknowledged leader of the Social Gospel in 1907 with the publication of *Christianity and the Social Crisis*. According to Walter Marshall Horton, ''The Social Gospel, with its hope of Christianizing the social order and building the Kingdom of God on earth was the main positive message of American liberalism before and during the First World War.'' [4]

Whereas on the Continent, the First World War led to a sharp crisis for liberal theology, signaled by Barth's commentary on Romans in 1919, in America

[4] Walter Marshall Horton, ''Systematic Theology,'' *Protestant Thought in the Twentieth Century*, ed. Arnold S. Nash (New York: Macmillan, 1951), p. 110.

liberal theology during the inter-war period was not
so much repudiated as it was modified. There was
no continuity of liberal theology in Europe com-
parable to that represented by theologians such as
A. C. Knudsen and E. S. Brightman at Boston University, Walter Marshall Horton at Oberlin, Harry
Emerson Fosdick in New York, William Adams
Brown and D. C. Macintosh at Yale, and above all
by the men at Chicago: E. S. Ames, Henry Nelson
Wieman and Shailer Mathews. The modification of
liberal theology occurred especially through the
work of the Niebuhr brothers who, while highly
critical of it, never repudiated it the way Barth,
Brunner, and Bultmann did on the Continent. Iron-
ically, however, liberalism as a whole was nonetheless disintegrating, partly because of the postwar
mood and partly because of the attacks of funda-
mentalism.[5] As a symptom of the confusion, one
may point to Shailer Mathews's own warning to the
religious education movement (the popular manifes-
tation of liberal Protestantism) that "it is our
privilege to teach young people that religion has
some other task than that of making good citizens
and good neighbors."[6]

With this brief introduction in mind, we can turn
now to Mathews himself. It will become evident that

[5] For a brief account, see Robert T. Handy, *The American Religious
Depression 1925–1935*, Facet Books, Historical Series (American
Church), 9 (Philadelphia: Fortress, 1968; reprint of *Church History*,
29 [1960], pp. 3–16). An excellent companion to Handy is *The Idea of
Progress in American Protestant Thought 1930–1960*, by Paul A.
Carter, Facet Books, Historical Series (American Church), 11 (Phila-
delphia: Fortress, 1969; reprint of *Church History*, 32 [1963], pp.
75–94).

[6] Shailer Mathews, "Let Religious Education Beware!" *The Christian Century* 44 (1927): 362.

he responded to both the intellectual and the social challenge of the day, becoming an important spokes- man for modernistic theology as well as for the Social Gospel. It was as spokesman for the latter that he wrote *Jesus on Social Institutions* in 1928 as the successor to *The Social Teachings of Jesus*, which had been published in 1897. Both testify to his abiding interest in the significance of the teachings of Jesus for the society of today and tomorrow.

MATHEWS'S LIFE AND CAREER

The life span of Shailer Mathews closely paral- leled the course of the liberal movement in the aca- demic tradition of American theology. Born in 1863, when Horace Bushnell had already introduced the basic motifs of liberal thinking, Mathews lived until 1941, when Reinhold Niebuhr's *The Nature of Man* appeared as a classic statement of a newly dominant neoorthodoxy. In the last decade of the nineteenth century, when Mathews was developing his socio- historical understanding of the Christian religion and abandoning the Baptist orthodoxy of his New England boyhood, liberal theology was becoming the major theological current in the leading intellectual centers of the country. Throughout the remainder of his life, Mathews was himself one of the leading exponents of liberalism. During a teaching career covering more than forty years, he contributed to the rise of the Social Gospel, wrote several impor- tant books in the field of New Testament history, and developed a distinctive theological perspective reflecting the tenets of "the Chicago School." At the heart of all of these efforts was his conviction that the Christian religion is a historical movement which has expressed its basic convictions in patterns derived from the various socio-cultural environments through which it has passed in the course of its development.

His studies at Colby College and Newton Theological Institution did little to disturb the evangelical piety inherited from his family. He did come to accept evolution during his college years, although Darwinism was generally regarded as inimical to the scriptural account of man's origin. Moreover, while in seminary he explored in an independent paper the idea that Paul's rabbinical thought may have carried over into his Christian writings, thus raising the question of historical relativity in relationship to the inspired text. However meager these beginnings may seem, they do mark a tendency to take seriously the implications of the natural and historical sciences for the interpretation of the Bible.

It was during two years of study in Berlin (1890–1892), however, that he developed an intellectual perspective that was to influence his academic labors for the rest of his career.[7] His principal mentors in Berlin were Hans Delbrück and Ignaz Jastrow in history and Adolf Wagner in economics. Delbrück and Jastrow instructed Mathews in the historiographical principles of Leopold von Ranke, the chief exponent of an objectivistic approach to writing history which endeavors to "tell it like it really was." According to this school, the historian's task is to study critically reliable primary sources in

---

[7] I am indebted to my colleague Kenneth L. Smith for an understanding of the importance of these years in Germany for the development of Mathews's methodology and outlook. See Kenneth L. Smith, *Shailer Mathews: Theologian of Social Process* (Ph.D. diss., Duke University, 1959), pp. 21–33.

order to ascertain the facts and demonstrate the relationships between important events. History so conceived is an autonomous discipline, completely independent of any *a priori* principles of philosophy or the dogmas of theology.

Wagner was one of the founders of the *Verein fur Sozialpolitik*, an organization devoted to the application of ethical principles to economic affairs. Their program repudiated *laissez-faire* capitalism, advocated social welfare supported by governmental action, and championed the interest of laboring people. Wagner, however, did not accept the socialistic principle that private property was to be abolished, although he contended that basic reforms in the prevailing capitalism were called for in the interest of society as a whole. His confidence that altruism was stronger than egoism provided the philosophical basis for his optimistic belief that ethical idealism could prevail in the marketplace.

Mathews was profoundly influenced by these German thinkers and made use of their ideas upon his return to America. Oddly enough, at this stage in life he was so devoted to history and social studies that he did not even hear a single lecture by the famous Adolf Harnack of Berlin. This detachment from theology he later regarded as fortunate since he learned objective historical research without any apologetic concerns for its results.

Mathews returned to Colby in 1892 and remained there for two more years. On the advice of Albion Small, who left Colby to go to the University of Chicago to establish the first graduate department of sociology in this country, Mathews began to read widely in this emerging field. The new sociology

which came to prominence in the last two decades of
the century under the dominating influence of Small
and Lester Ward regarded society as an organic
whole made up of interacting groups exhibiting
structural principles of sufficient definiteness to
make possible scientific study of social relationships.[8]
A strong inclination toward social reform and a
confidence in the teleological or rational direction of
society were characteristic of the founders of this
new discipline. Moreover, history itself was seen in
organic, evolutionary terms as a continuous process
of social interaction that shaped the development
of institutions and individuals. Hence, by the time
Mathews accepted a post in the Divinity School of
the University of Chicago (1894), the major intellectual influences that were to dominate his work as
a New Testament historian and theologian had
already taken root.

After twelve years in the department of New
Testament history, Mathews was transferred to the
field of Historical Theology, and in 1908 he became
Dean of the Divinity School. He remained as Dean
and taught courses in theology and ethics until his
retirement in 1933. During this period the Divinity
School of the University of Chicago was one of the
leading centers of theological inquiry in this country,
counting among its faculty some of the most dis-
tinguished names in the academic circles of American
Protestantism. In theology ''the Chicago School''
was characterized by strong left wing tendencies
which stressed the pragmatic and functional nature
of religious beliefs. Primary among its interests
was a search for a theological method oriented

[8] Ibid., pp. 34–44.

toward the natural and historical sciences and designed to uncover the abiding values of the Christian tradition. Naturalism, empiricism, and humanism, as well as pragmatism, figured prominently in the thinking of the theologians, while the socio-historical method dominated the approach of the biblical scholars. Eustace Haydon and Edward Scribner Ames developed religious philosophies on a naturalistic, humanistic, and pragmatic basis. George B. Foster agonized over the finality of Christianity. George Birney Smith wrestled with the cosmic aspects of the idea of God and applied the socio-historical method to the Christian past. J. M. P. Smith and Shirley Jackson Case worked in the field of biblical studies. Slightly later Henry Nelson Wieman developed his own version of empirical theology, a form of naturalistic theism based on a process model influenced by the philosophies of John Dewey and Alfred North Whitehead.

METHODOLOGY AND BASIC THEOLOGICAL PERSPECTIVE

At the center of "the Chicago School" was Shailer Mathews, whose writings dealt with New Testament history as well as with the reinterpretation of the Christian tradition for modern men. For Mathews the socio-historical method [9] served a twofold purpose. It provided a way of discovering the abiding values of the religion inaugurated by Jesus of Nazareth and a means of presenting them to modern man. Like all religions, Christianity, Mathews believed, arose to meet deep spiritual needs. Christianity attempts to fill these needs by its appeal to

[9] Ibid., pp. 49–88, for a detailed account of Mathews's understanding of the socio-historical method.

the way, the truth, and the life revealed in Jesus.
This persisting loyalty to Jesus gives continuity to
the Christian movement. But the intellectual framework in which Christian experience has been
expressed has changed from age to age. Doctrines
are functional formulas which come into being to
interpret the religious experience of the community.
Belief systems are relative to the socio-cultural
epoch in which they appear. The church appropri-
ates patterns current in the environing society and
uses them for theological purposes. Theology is, in
fact, "transcendentalized politics." This means that
religious beliefs are expressed in categories which
reflect the dominant social mind of a given cultural
epoch. Social mind is defined as "a more or less
general community of conscious states, processes,
ideas, interests, and ambitions which to a greater or
lesser degree repeats itself in the experience of individuals belonging to the group characterized by the
community of consciousness." [10] Christian theology,
then, is not an autonomous spiritual enterprise
developing in splendid independence of all conditioning factors. Rather, it gives intellectual legitimization to the religious experience of a community of
faith in conceptual forms that are relative not only
to other creative cultural enterprises like philosophy, literature, and science, but also to the total
complex of historical, economic, physical, and political factors which enter into the makeup of the social
order as a whole.

Mathews's thesis, as outlined above, has far-
reaching implications for the understanding of the

[10] Shailer Mathews, "Theology and the Social Mind," *The Biblical
World* 46 (October, 1915).

church and its message. First of all, it suggests that Christianity is a phase of the larger movement of Western civilization. "One can understand the history of Christianity only as a social eddy within the main current of the stream of history." [11] Moreover, theology is seen to be derived primarily from social experience and not philosophy. Theologians are more like social analysts than metaphysicians. Orthodoxy is simply the prevailing group consensus. Heresy, when more than individual opinion, is the formulation of a counter-social mind. Finally, theology is functional, not normative, changeable and not permanent. Theologies change with the social mind and must do so in order to be intelligible to succeeding generations. In short, Christianity is not to be studied as a body of dogmatic truth but as a religious social movement.

These convictions provide the clue to Mathews's grasp of the theological enterprise. The basic task of theology is to discover the relationships between the Christian movement and its social environment throughout its history and then to make use of these findings for the constructive work of articulating an adequate conceptual scheme for today. In general, then, the method Mathews employed involves two phases. The first consists of socio-historical research into the past. Here he made use of the historiographical tools and sociological insights gained in his early training to understand the interaction between the Christian movement and its cultural context through the centuries. Historical inquiry reveals that theology in every age is the articulation

[11] Edwin E. Aubrey, "Theology and the Social Process," *The Process of Religion*, ed. Miles Krumbine (New York: Macmillan, 1930), p. 12.

of group belief which serves the pragmatic task of relating religious experience to the totality of the socio-cultural ideology prevalent at a given time. The second step is to find categories in the contemporary social setting that can perform today the important function of rationalizing the experience and convictions of the community of believers. The employment of such a methodology is what Mathews called "modernism." Modernism is not primarily a name given to a specific set of theological beliefs standing over against traditional dogmas. Rather, it is defined as "the use of the methods of modern science to find, state, and use the permanent and central values of inherited orthodoxy in meeting the needs of a modern world."[12] To put it differently, "the use of scientific, historical, social method in understanding and applying evangelical Christianity to the needs of living persons is Modernism."[13]

Mathews concluded from his studies that Christianity has so far moved through seven successive social minds: the Semitic monarchical, which gave us the New Testament; the Graeco-Roman or Hellenistic monarchical, which gave us the ecumenical dogmas; the imperialistic, which gave us Latin Christianity; the feudal, which helped to fill out the content of divine imperialism; the nationalistic, which gave us Protestantism; the bourgeois, which gave us modern evangelicalism and Unitarianism; and the modern, which has contributed science and democracy. His thesis is that inquiry into the history of the church reveals that its institutional

[12] Shailer Mathews, *The Faith of Modernism* (New York: Macmillan, 1924), p. 23.

[13] Ibid., p. 35.

forms and doctrinal systems reflect the mentality generated by each of these social minds. The church now lives in an era dominated by empirical science and democratic social theory. Hence, if the church is to be relevant in this situation it must seek a positive accommodation with these basic ingredients of the contemporary mind.

The impact of democracy upon the modern world necessitates a rethinking of the traditional notion of divine sovereignty. The predominant pattern employed in the past to interpret the doctrine of God has been that of monarchy. At the present time, however, men demand a democratic God who recognizes the rights as well as the duties of men. Moreover, the old notion of a God who is not only transcendent but also external to the world, and who interferes arbitrarily with it from time to time, must be abandoned. Instead, God must be depicted as involved in the whole world process as its Resident Spirit and Immanent Purpose. Miracle in this new scheme loses its importance. The God of love becomes a God of law who works gradually and continually in an evolutionary fashion to achieve his goals. In *The Faith of Modernism* (1924) Mathews concludes that the modernist views God

> . . . as the undefined Person immanent in the universe in some such way as we finite persons are related to our bodies, upon whose good will humanity can rest in its anxieties and sorrows, its discontents and its aspirations; Who works in evolution and human history; Who is as loving and sympathetic as Jesus Christ; to Whom we can pray with full trust in His power; Who justifies our attempt to be loving; Who helps and transforms us.[14]

Here we have the outlines of a doctrine of God quite

[14] Ibid., pp. 120–121.

characteristic of the liberal theologians of this period—a democratic, mild-mannered, Jesus-like Power and Purpose immanent within the total cosmos and in human history working in a law-abiding way to create and perfect moral personality in man.

In the later years of his career Mathews turned increasingly to science as the most potent source of useful theological categories. This approach too was characteristic of the left wing liberals or modernists to whom method was the most important theological concern and for whom empirical science provided the enviable model which theologians should emulate to the limit that the subject matter would allow. Accordingly, two of Mathews's most important books are devoted to a reinterpretation of basic Christian concepts in the light of an organism-environment scheme taken from physics and biology. Science has shown the world to be a field of universal activity which is uniform throughout the realm of ascertainable fact. While no cosmic purpose as such can be proven, tendencies have appeared that are akin to what in the human sphere is called purposive. The most important such tendency has given rise to personality. The human self depends for its survival and fulfillment upon a proper adjustment with the total environment in which it flourishes. Religion comes into being to meet the needs of men in search of security and moral aid through a right relationship to whatever is the ultimate source of their being. Doctrines are intellectual hypotheses pertaining to normative religious adjustment. Conceptual schemes developed in encounter with the total cultural *Zeitgeist* are employed analogously in the moral and religious realms.

In *Atonement and the Social Process* (1930) Mathews works out this thesis in connection with a single basic theological idea. His conclusion is that in Christianity the mediating role between persons and the cosmic environment has been the person and work of Jesus. Over the centuries many different patterns have been employed, but they have all served the same function, namely, that of interpreting the meaning and method of forgiveness. Each successive doctrine of atonement has "endeavored not only to set forth God's saving, forgiving love, but also to meet objections against his moral right to forgive springing from contemporary practices."[15] God is thought in every case to offer forgiveness to men in accordance with commonly accepted procedures regarding rights, laws, honor, justice, sovereignty, and the like. Jesus is shown to perform whatever is required to make atonement possible. Having seen the functional value of these doctrines, Mathews sets forth his convictions regarding a contemporary equivalent. Man is a creature who has evolved out of nature over millions of years. His survival and fulfillment depend on a continuing adjustment with those processes in the cosmos which produced him. The traditional notion that God takes the initiative in salvation is said to mean that the personality-producing character of the cosmos is prior to man. Moreover, the co-working of man and the cosmic environment epitomizes the ancient claim that Jesus is both human and divine. Sin is deliberately chosen maladjustment with the nourishing

[15] Shailer Mathews, *Atonement and the Social Process* (New York: Macmillan, 1930), pp. 164–165.

processes inherent in the universe. This disharmony eventuates in suffering, guilt, and injustice. In this sense it was sin that led to the death of Jesus. The excellence of his example in remaining true to his conviction that love ultimately prevails is the power of the cross which assists others to attain unity with God. The resurrection points to the fact that Jesus triumphed over the suffering caused by the maladjustment of others to the personality-evolving forces of the cosmos because of his harmony with them.

Mathews turned next to the problem of the reality of God and the meaning of God-language. *The Growth of the Idea of God* (1931) carries forward the thesis that the concept of God is understood best through the history of its function in society rather than through metaphysical analysis. The notion of deity is not a philosophical absolute with some unchanging content. All ideas of God are relative to the needs and social mind-sets of various cultural eras. The meaning of God-language is to be found in the study of its actual usage by religious persons over the centuries. Moreover, there is no actual existing reality which corresponds exactly to any of the patterns which have been employed. Mathews argues, however, that his method does not dissolve the actuality of God into culturally relative ideas. Concepts of God express relationships between men and the cosmic environment which produced them, and only realities can be in relation. The patterns point to something objectively real even though the actuality of God is not literally described in any categorical scheme. God-language refers to "the person-

ality-evolving and personally-responsive activities
of the universe upon which human beings depend."[16]
Mathews called his view "conceptual theism."
While it does not allow us to think of God as an
individual Person, it is appropriate to use personal
models in that the cosmos is as a matter of fact
positively related to the production and perfection
of human personality. "Conceptual theism" is both
pragmatic and realistic in referring both to the
functional and practical significance of ideas of God
and in connecting concepts of deity with objective
actualities in the cosmic process. The advantages
of such a view, in Mathews's estimate, are that it provides confidence that human values are supported
by the cosmos, points to an objective grounding of
moral principles, and makes religion into a technique for attaining personal values and thus something more than conventional behavior.

The views held by Mathews concerning man and
his predicament also presuppose an evolutionary,
organic framework. Man is a free, purposive moral
being who has evolved from an animal background.
The fundamental human problem is that man's
emerging spirit is frustrated by the drag of natural
forces. His body is subject to mechanistic forces
(natural evil), and his spirit is weighted down by
the atavistic tendencies of his inherited animal passions. Sin is the consent of the will to the backward
pull of his bodily nature which seeks its own immediate pleasure. Salvation is the victory of the spirit
over the mechanisms of nature and the resistance of
untamed passions. This triumph occurs under the

[16] Shailer Mathews, *The Growth of the Idea of God* (New York: Macmillan, 1931), p. 219.

inspiration of Jesus and results in a life of trust in God and of goodwill toward other persons. Mathews was quite confident that man was gradually moving toward the realization of the ideals of Jesus in a universal kingdom of love and brotherhood. In *The Spiritual Interpretation of History* (1916) Mathews concludes that an inductive study of history supports the view that there are spiritual forces at work in history which, despite their conditioning by economic factors, are gradually bringing about an increase in personal values. Like everyone else Mathews was shocked by World War I but continued to believe until the end of his life that social evolution would carry man onward toward the perfection of historical existence.

What we have, then, in the thought of Shailer Mathews is a version of ethical-social modernism centering in the use of a socio-historical method for uncovering the inner meaning of the Christian past and in the use of patterns taken from contemporary science and democratic social thought to interpret the gospel for men in the present.

PROBLEMS POSED BY MATHEWS'S METHOD

Questions could profitably be raised regarding a whole range of issues in Mathews's thought, but only a few can be dealt with here. It is important, however, to give close attention to methodological problems before turning to particulars. Mathews's own claim was that modernism is primarily a method of interpretation and not essentially a new body of doctrines in competition with orthodoxy.

Methodological Problems. When subjected to critical examination, an inevitable tension becomes apparent between the social subjectivism inherent in his understanding of the socio-historical method and objectivistic elements associated with his appeal to Jesus of Nazareth and to the findings of historical research and modern science. The idea that theological doctrines are pragmatic, functional, and relative to a succession of cultural environments raises the question as to their truth content. Theology, contends Mathews, is the articulation of group religious belief in patterns taken from the larger society. In this framework Christianity is seen as the religion of all those who have considered themselves to be Christians, that is, loyal to Jesus of Nazareth. All of these convictions add up to a kind of culturally relative social subjectivism in which religious ideas are seen primarily from the point of view of their practical function of promoting the well-being of persons. One inevitably asks in this connection if there is any abiding ''essence'' which persists through all of these successive eras of Christian history. In what does the continuity of the message of the church lie? Is there any such unity? Or is Christianity simply identical with the history of its development, so that it is whatever it has become at a particular time and place? Theology is obviously correlated with the religious experience of the Christian community throughout the centuries, but in what way is it related to objective truths, realities, and values? On the other hand, Mathews assumes that the historical-critical method itself is not trapped in this cultural relativity; like others of his day, he minimizes virtually to the vanishing point the fact that the historian's portrait of the past is decisively affected by his own cultural setting no less than was the dogmatic tradition. In other words, we may formulate the methodological tension in the following way: whereas Mathews's social interpretation of history should have led him to emphasize that also the critical social-historical view of Christianity was but one of a series of relativities, he actually used the social-historical method over against the entire history of the tradition as if it stood outside it. It must be pointed out, however, that this attitude, largely unformulated, was what united him with liberal theology as a whole.

In moving toward a resolution of these questions, it is important to keep in mind that Mathews always presupposed the priority of experiences over belief.[17] The doctrine-making process has a natural history consisting of two components. The starting point is an experience of a new life in relationship to God and man. The second phase is the interpretation of this experience in the socially conditioned categories of a given environment. The continuity of the Christian movement is to be found in the moral and spiritual renewal of believers in successive generations. To use a phrase popularized by Harry Emerson Fosdick, Mathews speaks of "abiding experiences and changing categories."[18] Moreover, Mathews looked to the life, teaching, and personal example of the man Jesus as the source and norm of what is distinctive about the Christian religion.

[17] The priority of experience over doctrine was central also to Mathews's Continental contemporary, Wilhelm Herrmann (the liberal theologian who taught both Barth and Bultmann). See especially his *The Communion of the Christian with God*, to be published in this series, as introduced by Robert Voelkel.

[18] Harry Emerson Fosdick, *The Modern Use of the Bible* (New York: Macmillan, 1924), pp. 97–130.

xxxvi JESUS ON SOCIAL INSTITUTIONS

Given his confidence in the reliability of disinter-
ested historical research, he believed that a sufficiently detailed picture of Jesus and his teachings
could be arrived at to provide a basis for contemporary religious faith. What stands out in Jesus is
his total and consistent response of devotion to a
loving God and his dedication to the service of other
persons. The original impact of Jesus upon his disciples in evoking faith in God and love of neighbor
has been repeated continuously over the centuries,
resulting in the generation of certain basic convictions which constitute what Mathews often called
"generic Christianity." [19] While variously stated,
this core of essential affirmations revolves about the
redemptive transformation of individual and corporate life that is mediated through Jesus, eventuating
in the gradual, progressive establishing of a kingdom among men who are brothers to each other
because they are all sons of God.[20] However, in
addition to his insistence that there is an abiding
structure of interpreted Christian experience which
is the same from age to age, Mathews qualified the
social relativism of his position by making use of the
world picture generated by modern science. This
enabled him to speak of a pattern of cosmic activity
which resulted in the production of personality. This
provided an objective referent for the various ideas
of God, all of which reflected the changing mind of
the larger culture in which Christianity developed.
By taking up an organism-environment scheme from

[19] Shailer Mathews, "Generic Christianity," *Constructive Quarterly*
2 (December, 1914): 702–723.
[20] See, for example, Shailer Mathews, *The Gospel and Modern Man*
(New York: Macmillan, 1910), pp. 75–76; "Generic Christianity,"
pp. 719–720; *Modernism*, pp. 30–31.

biology, he found a contemporary way of schematizing the God-man-world relationship.

But now the question arises: To what extent do these considerations in fact qualify the subjectivism and pragmatic functionalism inherent in Mathews's thought? In the first instance, is not Mathews's own statement of ''generic Christianity'' simply another socially, historically, and individually conditioned interpretation of Christian truth and not a summary of core beliefs that could claim universal validity? Books written by Mathews about the life, teachings, messianic consciousness, and basic intentions of Jesus reflect a parochialism of time, place, and point of view as surely as any others found elsewhere in other centuries and cultures. Assuming the principles of the socio-historical method, one inevitably confronts a dilemma. One can frame Christian truth in statements achieving a high level of generality and universality at the expense of specific, detailed content. Or one can aim at concreteness and particularity by giving up the goal of wide generality of application. Mathews does not seem to have transcended these limits. At best he attained some kind of happy middle ground between these extremes. Again, is there in fact an identifiable structure of Christian experience which persists throughout the centuries? What common features belong to Christian existence as experienced by a member of the church at Corinth to whom Paul wrote, a medieval mystic in a monastic community, an American frontiersman in the nineteenth century, and a scientific modernist of 1925? Granted that there is in each case the formal assertion of the ultimacy of Jesus as the source of salvation, in concrete terms how much further can one go in specifying universal features of Christian redemption? There are undoubtedly some pervasive elements of experienced faith, hope, and love which do spring from the inner nature of the Christian gospel. The only question is whether or not Mathews's own version of "generic" or "primary" Christianity is sufficiently valid or free enough from relativity to justify the confidence which he apparently invested in it.

A similar problem arises with respect to his use of scientific language to give objective content to the doctrine of God. Is the utilization of the organism-environment model and his conception of God in terms of the personality-producing factors in the cosmos simply another instance of social subjectivism? Are these categories the expression of a contemporary social mind which will in time fade away in favor of models generated by some future social mind? Or has Mathews found a way out of relativism by means of empirical science? Do we really know now what previous theologies have grasped only vaguely since they lacked the evolutionary viewpoint provided by scientific knowledge? Mathews's reliance on the socio-historical method led him to classify scientific analogies along with all the other patterns of previous theologies, while his confidence in science as a dependable means of obtaining objective knowledge about the world led him to affirm the transcultural validity of its conclusions. To be sure, Mathews nowhere claimed that science gives us a precise, systematically complete ontological description of the inner being and essence of God, since such knowledge is apparently not possible for men. Still, he maintained that science has at least uncovered the objective referent of God-language. More-over, Mathews claimed to have discovered the formal pattern into which all ideas of deity fit. But does this formal pattern filled with the concrete content furnished by empirical science with its evolutionary scheme provide a fund of reliable, objective knowl-edge which is any more permanent or less relative than that found in previous theologies lacking what Mathews's research uncovered? If the answer is yes, then Mathews has, in some limited degree, by the use of science, transcended the social subjectiv-ism which is otherwise so pervasive. If the answer is negative, then his own constructive thought is as thoroughly relative as other theological systems. In this case, one has to make the same distinction in Mathews's writings between ''generic Christianity'' and its contingent, secondary, cultural features that he made in respect to past theologies.

Mathews's Particular Emphases. Turning now to the specifics of his thought, let us examine first Mathews's conception of God. Concern with the theology of Mathews was gradually eclipsed in the years following 1930 by the increasing strength of neoorthodoxy.[21] Methodologically, this movement focused attention on the Bible and the Protestant Reformers as sources of theology which provided the necessary corrective to the alleged deficiencies of the culturally-based revisionist doctrines of liberal-ism. Hence, neoorthodox theologians stressed the freedom, sovereignty, and transcendence of the Lord Almighty; thereby they opposed the reductive ten-dencies of the evolutionary, immanental theism of the liberals.

[21] See *The Impact of American Religious Liberalism,* chapter 12.

Today, on the contrary, there is a potential openness to the thought of Mathews that was not present
ten or twenty years ago. For example, no problem is
more central in recent theology than the meaning
and relevance of language about deity.[22] The conceptual theism of Mathews was designed to speak of
God in Christian fashion to the increasingly secular-
ized scientific mentality of modern men. Mathews
agreed with the many who today hold that this task
requires the radical reconstruction of traditional
modes of thought. Moreover, Mathews's attempt to
discover the nature of God-talk by studying its
actual use in common practice is a theme made
familiar by theologians currently under the influence
of linguistic analysis. There is much agreement also
between many of these thinkers and the view of
Mathews that theological language is fundamentally
expressive of internal commitments and experiences
and does not consist first of all of metaphysical
assertions about transcendent realities. At any
rate, his discussion of the pragmatic, functional,
existential aspects of God-language in relationship
to the metaphysical, cognitive, theoretical dimensions has much in common with the current conversation. Moreover, Mathews's concern to relate the
Christian understanding of God to the organic
processes of an evolving cosmos as well as to history
converges with emphases central to process theol-

[22] For accounts of the theological impact of linguistic philosophy, see
Frederick Ferre, *Language, Logic and God* (New York: Harper, 1961),
and William Hordern, *Speaking of God* (London: Macmillan, 1964).
Extensive reference to the philosophical and theological literature will
be found in these volumes.

ogy, now resurging into prominence.[23] In short, there is a contemporaneity about some of the methods and motifs of conceptual theism which would not have been acknowledged at the height of the neoorthodox period.

The basic criticisms leveled by neoorthodoxy have already been alluded to. From the standpoint of a contemporary process theologian three deficiencies of Mathews's doctrine of God come immediately to mind. First of all, he had a deep animus against philosophy, and metaphysics in particular. Philosophical systems were, he contended, the products of individual minds engaged in speculation. He disliked this approach because he believed theology should be grounded in group religious experience and because he had been influenced by the positivistic critiques of Comte and Spencer. However, this neglect of the values inherent in careful critical conceptual analysis resulted in confusion, shallowness, and obscurity. There are metaphysical implications in his assertions which he was not prepared to clarify or defend. A process theologian naturally is inclined to think that categories such as those provided by the dipolar theism of Charles Hartshorne, for example, enable him to preserve, in some measure at least, the freedom and transcendence of God, which the neoorthodox contended for, as well as the immanent working of God within nature to produce

---

[23] For example, see John Cobb, *A Christian Natural Theology* (Philadelphia: Westminster, 1965), Schubert Ogden, *The Reality of God* (New York: Harper, 1966), and Richard Overman, *Evolution and the Christian Doctrine of Creation* (Philadelphia: Westminster, 1967). I count myself in this general group, although my own point of view is more naturalistic and therefore closer to Mathews than the three authors cited here.

and sustain personality. At a minimum, careful attention to precise analysis would have made it possible for his readers to decide just what the evolutionary theistic naturalism indicated by his conceptual view of God really did imply. Again, his discussion of the nature and function of religious language could have been sharpened, clarified, and made more conceptually adequate by greater attention to and appropriation of the critical tools of philosophical inquiry.

A second criticism is closely related to the first. The claim that God is the concept men have of the personality-producing activities in the cosmos appears to be an attempt to designate the logical, formal, generic meaning of the term common to all doctrines in distinction to the specific material content of particular formulations. The difficulty is that the category of ''personality-producing factors in the universe'' is too concrete to serve the requirements of the former and too abstract to be sufficient for the latter without more clarification. Here again attention to and use of the conceptual tools provided by careful philosophical analysis could have assisted Mathews in clarifying his views as well as in making them more adequate. God as a final referent word serving as the category of the ultimate in metaphysics and religion requires an analysis more complete and precise than Mathews gives. The concept of personality-producing factors needs to be connected with a cosmology worked out in more detail and connected both with scientific and metaphysical perspectives. He was neither interested in nor equipped to do what was required to make his conception of God both clear and conceptually adequate.

Finally, Mathews's view of God is deficient in its dealing with the problem of evil. There is an imperturbably sanguine optimism on the pages of his works that does not square with the enormity or the agony of physical and moral evil. The attempt to interpret natural evil in terms of the connections between the organic structures of the body and the impersonal mechanisms of physics and chemistry obscures the depth and complexity of animal and human suffering, although this is certainly part of the total truth. Moral evil is related too simply to the atavistic drag of animal impulse. Mathews's conception of the human predicament sounds shallow in comparison with the theologies informed by depth psychology and existential philosophy, although no finality is hereby claimed for either of these. The point is that God seems to confront obstacles to the fulfillment of his purposes in the cosmos as well as in the human self more profound and complex than Mathews ever envisioned. My own view is that an evolutionary theism based on a process model requires the doctrine of a suffering, struggling God whose loving will contends against some dark primordial impediment which vitiates the purposive processes of nature and history. At any rate, many who could not accept my view would join me in judging the outlook of Mathews to be too simple and sentimental in the face of the giant agonies of our time.

With regard to Mathews's doctrine of man a briefer word is in order. Neoorthodoxy focused attention on the perversity of the self's radical freedom in its accounts of the origin of sin. Evolutionary views of man were accepted as biologically true but largely theologically irrelevant. Man's behavior was understood primarily from the standpoint of his self-transcending spirit.[24] While there is profound truth here that must not be forgotten, the evolutionary perspective of Mathews with its use of an organism-environment scheme also has some validity which neoorthodoxy neglected. Mathews correctly saw the value of viewing man within the total cosmic, biological, and historical context in which he comes to be. Contemporary perspectives remind us that man is a biospiritual creature who needs to be understood in the light of biology and genetics as well as in terms of biblical mythology and existential phenomenology. Neoorthodox analyses of man run the risk of being abstract, acosmic, and ahistorical in that the object of analysis tends to be a free, transcendent self, wrenched from the total organic, evolutionary, biogenetic context in which it comes into being.[25] Doubtless neither the

[24] The classical American statement of neoorthodoxy is found in Reinhold Niebuhr, *The Nature and Destiny of Man*, 1 vol. ed. (New York: Scribner's, 1949). See Vol. 1, pp. 150–500, for his positive statement of man as immersed in nature and yet transcendent to it. See Vol. 1, pp. 18–122, for a critique of faulty modern views of man. See also *Faith and History* (New York: Scribner's, 1949), pp. 70–101. Finally, see *The Self and the Dramas of History* (New York: Scribner's, 1955), pp. 105–182 for a criticism of naturalistic and evolutionary views of history.

[25] In the case of Reinhold Niebuhr it was not that he ignored or disregarded the biological and organic dimensions of selfhood but simply that he was so under the influence of human self-transcendence that he did not make sufficient theological usage of the information from the biological sciences that was available to him. He was in reaction to a simplistic biological explanation of moral evil. He was concerned to locate sin in the freedom of the human spirit and not in the drag of man's animal nature. Moreover, new data from the behavioral sciences have come to light that this generation of theologians must make use of. John Cobb's *The Structure of Christian Existence*, (Philadelphia: Westminster, 1967), is a first step in providing a framework in which this new theological work can go on.

evolutionary biologism found in Mathews nor the existentialist spiritism of neoorthodoxy is adequate for the future. What is called for is a comprehensive theology of life informed by the natural, social, and behavioral sciences which will result in a practical theory of biopolitics, i.e., concrete strategies for preserving, enhancing, and fulfilling the human potentiality for enjoyment and ecstasy.[26] A biopolitical theology views life within its total cosmohistorical, biocultural, sociotechnological setting and can be useful to man in his quest for the good future. My point here is that the theology of today and tomorrow can learn from Shailer Mathews as well as from Reinhold Niebuhr as it seeks to move beyond both to a view of human nature and destiny more adequate than either ever achieved.

With this general analysis and evaluation in mind, let us turn now directly to those writings of Mathews that deal with the quest to understand the life and work of Jesus.

THE LIFE AND TEACHINGS OF JESUS

The earliest writings of Mathews dealing with the life of Jesus were concerned with what he called "Christian sociology." It has already been indicated that one of the formative influences on his developing thought was the new sociology of men like Albion Small and Lester Ward. This was an organic-process oriented study motivated by ethical idealism directed toward social reform. Mathews was impressed with the important role which sociology could play in relation to the church and its mis-

---

[26] See my article, "The Case for Christian Biopolitics," *The Christian Century* 86 (1969): 1481–83.

sion. At the beginning of his career he also felt that this emerging new discipline could be guided by the teaching of the New Testament. Indeed, Christian truth could, if the opportunity were properly exploited, become the greater part of social philosophy and thus exert a powerful directive toward the development of a higher civilization. Sociology could study the actual structures and processes of social institutions, but it needed normative criteria. For Mathews, social norms were to be derived from the teachings of Jesus. The result is "Christian sociology," by which he meant "the social philosophy and teachings of the historical person, Jesus the Christ." [27] Later on, Mathews spoke instead of the Social Gospel, which attempted to apply the teachings of Jesus to the needs of the new industrial society. [28]

In 1897 Mathews published what was probably his most popular book under the title *The Social Teachings of Jesus*. He gave it the subtitle "An Essay in Christian Sociology." Appearing originally as a series of articles in the *American Journal of Sociology*, the book was continually reprinted until 1928 when it was replaced by *Jesus on Social Institutions*. In his autobiography Mathews maintains that when it appeared originally in 1897, it was the first volume in English in its field. [29] Frederick C. Grant has endorsed this estimate, suggesting further that *The Social Teachings of Jesus* "had an immense influ-

[27] Shailer Mathews, *The Social Teachings of Jesus* (New York: Macmillan, 1897), p. 3.

[28] Shailer Mathews, *The Social Gospel* (Philadelphia: The Griffith and Roland Press, 1910).

[29] Shailer Mathews, *New Faith for Old* (New York: Macmillan, 1936), p. 120.

ence, especially here in America, where for a generation and longer it was one of the two or three major
textbooks of the social-gospel school of New Testament interpretation."[30]

In retrospect Mathews concludes that although its
continued sale argued for its usefulness, this work
represented a type of biblical interpretation which
can now be seen to be inadequate. Specifically what
he meant was that the book contained "what might
be called a transitional view of the kingdom of God
as a social order to be reached progressively."[31]
Later, he came to see that the concept was eschatological. He rewrote the book and issued it again as
Jesus on Social Institutions. It will be instructive to
trace the development of Mathews's views in this
connection and to see how he employed the socio-
historical method to deal with the apocalyptic setting
of the ethical teachings of Jesus.

Let us examine first the conception of the kingdom
of God which appears in *The Social Teachings of
Jesus*. Jesus does not mean, Mathews contends, a
"merely political kingdom or theocratic state."[32]
Neither does he have in mind "a perfect method of
life for the individual."[33] Mathews then refers to,
but finally rejects, the idea that the kingdom of God
is an apocalyptic concept. Mathews's own conclusion is: "By the kingdom of God Jesus meant *an
ideal* (though progressively approximated) *social
order in which the relation of men to God is that*

[30] Frederick C. Grant, "Ethics and Eschatology in the Teachings of
Jesus," *The Journal of Religion* 22 (October, 1942): 359.

[31] Mathews, *New Faith*, p. 120.

[32] Mathews, *Social Teachings*, p. 44.

[33] Ibid., pp. 45–46.

of sons, and (therefore) *to each other, that of
brothers.*"[34] This divine brotherhood is the "goal
of social evolution."[35] Such an ideal society is not
beyond historical attainment but is "the natural
possibility for man's social capacities and powers."[36]
The optimism inherent in this conception is apparent. Mathews believed that the kingdom of God

[34] Ibid., p. 54. In this book, Mathews is aware of Johannes Weiss's
portrayal of Jesus as influenced definitively by apocalyptic. At the
same time, he seeks a way to blend the idealistic reading of the kingdom
with the eschatological. Thus, immediately after the definition quoted
above, he wrote, "The point of departure . . . must be the historical
expectation of the Jews in the days of Jesus" (p. 55). Having sketched
this, he wrote, "He took the hope as he found it. He never needed to
define it. He had simply to correct and elevate the immanent idea. The
Christian kingdom is the Jewish kingdom, but transfigured and made
universal by the clarifications of Jesus" (p. 57 f.).

[35] Ibid., p. 75. Mathews held that "Jesus in his double revelation of
God to man and humanity to man inaugurated its historical life" (p.
72). ". . . the kingdom is thought of by Jesus as present as well as
future, and that its history is an evolution. Each stage of the growth
will be to a considerable degree determined by the character of the men
—of groups of men—with whom the new order has to deal" (p. 73).

[36] Ibid., p. 77. Speaking of Jesus entrusting the future of the kingdom to his disciples, Mathews wrote, "The audacity of Jesus in assuming that a group of such men had within it the possibility of indefinite
expansion is equalled only by the superb optimism that saw possibilities
of infinite good in humanity. In both lay his philosophy of the growth
of the new social order. If his teaching had been less human and humanity less capable of moral rebirth, he would have been but one of the
motley crew of Christs who have so often appeared only to delude and
destroy" (p. 201).
Nevertheless, Mathews has not surrendered the apocalyptic completely. "Yet a startling thing in this calm anticipation of a slow and
painful process is his recognition of the possibility of a time when the
forces of human nature should be insufficient; when the new social
order would be so far established as to have transformed and assimi-
lated all of the transformable material it found in its environment.
Until that time, of necessity the two opposing worlds must have existed
side by side. . . . Then, through some exercise of the supreme power of
the heavenly Father and King, the agony and the transformation were
to cease together. . . . As to when this supplementing of growth by
cataclysm shall come, Jesus gives us no information. But that he should
have seen the necessity of it is a tribute to his sense of reality"
(p. 227 f.).

would gradually come into reality as men were inspired by Jesus to emulate the character and life which they found in him. The motive power of the new life of love is the disclosure mediated through Jesus of sonship to God. If men come to know that they are indeed heir to God's love, then they can begin to love the neighbor as a brother.[37] Here the gospel is presented as essentially a simple moral idealism which presupposes that man is basically an altrustic innocent easily lured into the higher life.

In *A History of New Testament Times* (1899) the kingdom of God is again represented as an ideal social order on earth in which men obey the divine will while living as sons of God and brothers to each other.[38]. But by 1905 when he published *The Messianic Hope in the New Testament* Mathews had changed his mind. He now viewed the kingdom of God in eschatological terms as a radically new order of things to be given to the righteous by divine action, not achieved by the progressive idealization of society through human effort.

> Any strict definition of the kingdom of God as used by Jesus must be eschatological. With Jesus as with his contemporaries the kingdom was yet to come. Its appearance would be the result of no social evolution, but sudden, as the gift of God; men could not hasten its coming; they could only prepare for membership in it.[39]

Frederick C. Grant has said also of this 1905 book that it was "a pioneer work, without which, at least

[37] Ibid., pp. 186–202.

[38] Shailer Mathews, *A History of New Testament Times in Palestine* (New York: Macmillan, 1899), pp. 171–172.

[39] Shailer Mathews, *The Messianic Hope in the New Testament* (Chicago: The University of Chicago Press, 1905), p. 82.

in this country and Great Britain, the independent growth of the 'eschatological interpretation' might not have taken place.''[40] Mathews gives us few clues regarding the considerations that led him to revise his earlier views concerning the eschatological element in the teachings of Jesus. Two books are usually referred to as most decisive in bringing about the triumph of the view that the kingdom of God in the thought of Jesus is a future reality which will be established imminently by the direct action of God at the close of the present age. These epoch-making volumes are *Die Predigt Jesu vom Reiche Gottes* (1892) by Johannes Weiss and *Vom Reimarus zu Wrede* (1906) by Albert Schweitzer.[41] In *The Social Teachings of Jesus* Mathews refers twice to the former work but rejects Weiss's apocalyptic interpretation of the kingdom.[42] *The Messianic Hope in the New Testament* was published the year before *Vom Reimarus zu Wrede*. Mathews never went as far as either Weiss or Schweitzer in stressing the futuristic aspects of the kingdom of God. Instead he held to a view which recognized the present reality of the divine reign as well as the consummation which was yet to come. However, on the basic point after 1905 Mathews asserted the

[40] Grant, ''Ethics and Eschatology in the Teachings of Jesus,'' p. 359.

[41] The English translation of Schweitzer's book was published under the title *The Quest of the Historical Jesus* (London: Macmillan, paperback ed., 1961). The first (1892) edition of Weiss's book, translated for the first time, is included in this series: *Jesus' Proclamation of the Kingdom of God*, trans. and ed. D. Larrimore Holland and Richard H. Hiers (Philadelphia: Fortress, 1971). Weiss's second, expanded edition of 1900, was reissued in 1964 by Vandenhoeck & Ruprecht in Göttingen.

[42] See note 34. It should be noted that Mathews did not reject outright Weiss's interpretation but its thoroughgoing application to Jesus.

priority of the eschatological dimension. The question "is no longer one of adjusting the eschatological teachings to his religio-sociological, but that of adjusting his references to a present kingdom to his entire eschatological scheme."[43] Writing a half century later, Rudolf Bultmann remarks:

> Today nobody doubts that Jesus' conception of the Kingdom of God is an eschatological one—at least in European theology and, as far as I can see, also among American New Testament scholars. Indeed, it has become more and more clear that the eschatological expectation and hope is the core of the New Testament preaching throughout.[44]

The recognition of the apocalyptic setting of the concept of the kingdom of God left Mathews with the problem of interpreting its contemporary relevance, given the fact that the expected end of the age did not occur. Mathews takes up this question in some detail in *The Messianic Hope in the New Testament*. His employment of the socio-historical method leads him as always to distinguish between the form and the content of an inherited doctrine. There are universal, permanent truths and values which belong to the eternal gospel which can be separated from the socially conditioned form of expression in which they appear in the New Testament. For example, the eschatological scheme cannot be accepted literally but it does contain two abiding notes of religious truth: the conviction that the good man will survive death and that God will assist those who trust him.[45] Moreover, while Jesus' ideas of the kingdom of God

[43] Mathews, *Messianic Hope*, p. 80.

[44] Rudolf Bultmann, *Jesus Christ and Mythology* (New York: Scribner's, 1958), p. 13.

[45] Mathews, *Messianic Hope*, p. 121.

were set within the framework of Jewish messianism, there are important ways in which he transformed the entire conception. Jesus purified the
ethical requirements of the kingdom, saw God consistently as a loving Father and not as a stern
Judge, rejected the military and political connota-
tions of the messianic title Son of David, universal-
ized the coming kingdom, and taught that he as
messiah must suffer, die, and be resurrected.[46] The
most important consideration, however, is the messianic self-consciousness of Jesus. Jesus was conscious of being so constantly and perfectly indwelt
by the Spirit and of having such an intimate, unique
relationship to God as to constitute a veritable divine
incarnation. So great was his consciousness of this
divine status that nothing less than the highest possible valuations available among his people would
suffice to express it. Not only would he perform all
the wonders associated with the consummation of
the kingdom in his role as the eschatological Son of
man, but his own position as the exalted Christ took
priority over the kingdom itself. In short, the essential element to which all else is subordinate is Jesus
himself.[47] "This personality rather than its interpretation is, especially in its twofold historical revelation of God-in-man and of the resurrection, the
first great essential of the Christian gospel."[48]
Through Jesus there has been mediated an experience of a loving, forgiving God that results in a new
life of self-sacrificing love toward the neighbor,
undergirded by a confident hope of immortal life in

[46] Ibid., pp. 108–119.
[47] Ibid., pp. 120–133.
[48] Ibid., p. 318.

the world to come. "This new life, rather than its interpretation, is the second essential verity of the Christian gospel."[49] Mathews concludes:

In a word, to remove or to allow for messianism is not to destroy the essentials of the gospel—the personality, the teaching, and the resurrection of Jesus; a rational faith in God as Father; a certainty of divine forgiveness; an experience of the eternal life; an assurance of a complete life beyond and because of death. It is rather to make them more intelligible, more convincing, more certain, and more dynamic.[50]

THE SOCIAL GOSPEL OF JESUS

Nearly a quarter of a century later Mathews takes up these same issues again and offers in *Jesus on*

[49] Ibid.

[50] Ibid., p. 321. Since this series includes the influential book by Wilhelm Herrmann, *The Communion of the Christian with God*, it is useful to compare the adjustment of this liberal theologian to the eschatological character of Jesus' mission with that of Mathews. Herrmann's adjustment appears in the essay "The Moral Teachings of Jesus" which is included in *Essays on the Social Gospel* by Adolf Harnack and Wilhelm Herrmann, trans. G. M. Craik and ed. M. A. Canney (London: Williams & Norgate, 1907). Referring to the 2d ed. of Johannes Weiss's epoch-making study of the proclamation of Jesus, Herrmann says that the discovery of the eschatological horizon does indeed show that Jesus' words give us no clear directions in our situation. But this is a great benefit, because it prevents a perfectionist imitation of Jesus (pp. 176 ff.), such as exemplified by Tolstoy. But Herrmann is not content with this, for he cannot leave Jesus totally under the aegis of apocalyptic. Consequently, he also argued that one cannot contend "that it is mainly in the anticipation of the approaching end of the world that the key is to be found to those words of Jesus which run counter to the way of thinking common among men . . . the characteristic note in the words of Jesus is due above all to His intentness upon the eternal goal. . . ." After referring to Jesus' teaching on love, he asks, "Could Jesus have been induced to take such a view by the imminence of the end of the world, and of judgment?" (p. 202 f.). Finally, he turns the phenomenology of Jesus' life into a moral maxim which is essentially historical: "With regard to these utterances of Jesus (about indifference to the world) we confess that we cannot possibly comply with them, since we do not share His conception of the universe, and so are living in a different world. On the other hand, the mind which they reveal should be present also in us; that is, the will ready to act in accordance with our own convictions" (p. 207).

Social Institutions his latest conclusions about the Social Gospel of Jesus in terms of its meaning and relevance for contemporary society.

By observing how Mathews rewrote *The Social Teachings of Jesus*, we can detect subtle shifts in perspective. Structurally, the two books are quite dissimilar. Not only is the subtitle, "An Essay in Christian Sociology," deleted from the later work, but the topics in each of the nine-chapter books are apportioned differently. In *The Social Teachings*, the chapters are: Introduction (relating Jesus' teaching to "Christian sociology" as "the social philosophy and teachings of the historical person Jesus the Christ"), Man (biblical anthropology, with accent on man's capacities for relationships), Society (the kingdom of God as an ideal social order), The Family, The State, Wealth, Social Life, The Forces of Human Progress, and the Process of Social Regeneration. The Preface to the new book reports that it was the study of the French Revolution which convinced Mathews of the importance of social psychology for the study of Jesus. Accordingly, new chapters appear: The Revolutionary Spirit in the Time of Jesus, Jesus and the Revolutionary Spirit, Jesus on Social Attitudes, Jesus as the Exponent of Social Attitudes; then follow chapters on the family, wealth and the state which he rewrote but slightly; new are the chapters on Jesus and the Church, and The Social Gospel of Jesus.

Upon closer examination, it is apparent that the chapter on Jesus as the Exponent of Social Attitudes is essentially the earlier chapter, Social Life, for which he has written a new introduction (p. 65 f.) and conclusion. What he omitted was answers to the

charge that Jesus was not a preacher of social equality because he discriminated against Samaritans.
Similarly, the chapter on the family is given a new
introduction and conclusion, plus a more complete
battery of footnotes. The new conclusion is more
concerned with the contemporary import of Jesus'
teachings. The chapter on wealth implies a fascinat-
ing shift in perspective. Whereas the earlier discussion began by emphasizing the importance of
seeing how great was Jesus' concern for problems
of wealth, the new chapter begins by fending off
those who take this to extremes—Kalthoff and
other socialist interpreters of Jesus. Jesus was not
a reformer but a "herald of a moral attitude."
Still, the statement that Jesus is close to the general
position of socialism is allowed to stand. On the
other hand, apparently both Mathews's research
and his observations during the postwar decade led
him to say now what he had not said in 1897: "A
declaration of rights is a precursor of civil war"
(p. 107). From the previous chapter on the state
Mathews deleted the sketch of the history of Christian attitudes toward the state; in its place stands a
discussion of Jesus the nation-minded Jew. The
new conclusion is much more ample, again devoted
to the effect of appropriating Jesus' attitude today.
On pp. 114 ff. Mathews relates the spirit of Jesus to
current efforts to outlaw war, while at the same time
legitimating the "just war" theory. Mathews also
insists that there is a fundamental difference
between Christianizing men and Christianizing government (p. 118), a note of realism about institutions lacking in *The Social Teachings*.

The shifts in historical perspective (regarding the importance of eschatology for Jesus) are easier to ascertain than shifts in overall outlook. That Mathews became more ''conservative'' in his own understanding of social change is not altogether clear, though one can point to certain statements in the present volume that might suggest it. The very fact that he wrote a new chapter on the church suggests a growing awareness that the leaven of Jesus' social ideal works through an institution (p. 135 f.), as does the content of the chapter. Still, he insists that ''in the last analysis social progress is not a matter of systems but of folks'' because ''men cannot gather social figs from individual thistles'' (p. 130 f.). Mathews's reasoning is not difficult to discern: as Jesus' teaching was ''intended to evoke an attitude of soul'' (p. 125), so ''the church is a social institution in which group life is being educated in goodwill'' (p. 134). Thus Mathews is concerned to nurture the ''revolutionary attitude,'' not to launch or even encourage revolutions. This note of the primacy of persons remains in both volumes. In *The Social Teachings*, he distinguished between individualism and atomism (p. 210) in order to be able to insist that because reformations do not proceed en masse, ''there must be the successive winning of one man after another until there be developed something like a nucleus of a more perfect social life'' (p. 211). In 1897 he also wrote, ''It cannot be too often emphasized that social regeneration according to the conception of Christ cannot proceed on any other line than that of replacing bad men by good men. And this above all is the function of the church. . . . To aid in the regeneration of a man is to aid in the regeneration of society" (p. 224 f.). Consequently, Christian social efforts "can never remove the need for the older and more permanent work of the missionary" (p. 224). In the present volume, the role of the church as institutionalizing the attitude of Jesus (p. 137) is given prominence not found in the earlier book. This is his way of reasserting the primary religious task of the church, a point scored against the more extreme forms of the Social Gospel (cf. p. 143).

If the earlier book was more influential and the later, though more sober, had less impact, it may have been because the former was not only a pioneer work but an expression of the optimism of the day while the latter emerged amid the growing disarray of liberalism. Today some might accuse him of equivocating on the issue of revolution, partly because of his own attitudes and partly because one might ask whether it is sufficient to relate only the teachings of Jesus to the revolutionary currents of his day. Actually, not only must the career and execution of Jesus be understood in this light but one should inquire whether his teachings themselves do not have the concrete situation in Palestine in mind more than even Mathews allows.

While the details are available in the full text which follows this introduction, it may be useful at this point to indicate how Mathews deals with the issues of ethics in relation to eschatology—a subject still very much with us today.[51]

[51] In addition to the now classical book by Amos Wilder, *Eschatology and Ethics in the Teachings of Jesus* (New York: Harper, rev. ed. 1950; 1st ed. 1939), see Richard H. Hiers, *Jesus and Ethics* (Philadelphia: Westminster, 1968), where the views of Harnack, Schweitzer, Bultmann and Dodd are discussed.

At the outset it should be noted that this volume displays a characteristic feature of the socio-historical method. From the opening chapter onward the underlying assumption is that men and events of the past can best be understood when they are seen within the larger cultural whole to which they belong. A wide frame of reference is required which relates the particular object of study to the social dynamics operative within a given region and era. An organic-process view of history and society is at work here that prompts the historian to look for the total configuration resulting from the interplay of the relevant psychological, economic, political, religious, intellectual, and other cultural factors which are at work in a given setting. When Mathews looked at the period in which Jesus lived, he concluded that the social psychology of revolution provided the best clue to that constellation of factors which constituted the dominant historical reality of that age. Hence, this framework was adopted for the purpose of reconstructing Jesus' life and teachings. It is within this context also that the messianic hope is approached. The longing for the radical transformation of society was pervasive. One form of this dream was a faith in the nearness of a great upheaval that would put an end to the present social order and establish a fundamentally new one. Jesus appropriated this version of the messianic vision, expressing his convictions in the rhetoric of apocalypticism. Moreover, he believed himself to be the long awaited deliverer through whom God would act to give the kingdom to the saints.

In the light of this apocalyptic orientation, how are we to understand the relationship between eschatology and ethics? How did Jesus view the connection between the divine gift of the new age and the human response prerequisite to enjoying its blessings? And how do the ethical teachings with respect to social issues fit into the expectation of an imminent end to all worldly institutions? Three basic points need to be made in this connection. First of all, while Jesus adopted a contemporary set of ideas regarding the near end of the present age and the breaking in of the new order by God's direct intervention, he transformed them in the light of his own insights and experience. What stands out in bold relief is the startling clarity with which love is made central to theology and ethics. God is a loving Father who demands that men love one another. The consistency with which Jesus expressed in word and deed this vision of the God-man relationship provides a clue to his person and ministry. The second point grows out of the first. The primary frame of reference for the ethical teachings of Jesus is not the eschatological hope of a divinely wrought revolution in human history but the character and will of God. There is an absolute, timeless element at the root of the moral demands of Jesus. The unchanging standard of right human behavior is the recognition that the ultimate fact of existence is the goodwill of God extended toward man and expected of man. Hence, there may be interim mores in the teachings of Jesus but no interim ideal.[52] Men must

[52] In this way, Mathews grants Schweitzer his point but deprives it of its import; that is, by working with the category of permanent truth and temporal expression, he is able to say that the particulars Jesus demanded were determined by the interim (Schweitzer's ''interim ethic''), but that the timeless ideal was the character of God. It is instructive to compare this solution with that advanced by Wilder (see note 51).

love others because God loves and demands love. The ideal of sacrificial social-mindedness which regards persons as ends and not means and which seeks the good of another is a moral absolute grounded in the reality and purpose of God. Finally, love of neighbor expressed in acts and attitudes appropriate for the ideal social order envisioned by Jesus is not the condition for bringing the kingdom of God into being but the condition for enjoying its blessings. Jesus was not engaged in social reform by urging men to act in certain ways that would lead toward desirable change. Rather his teachings provide illustrations of what human conduct guided by the absolute moral ideal would be like. The specific ethical teachings are to be understood in the light of the unqualified imperative of love which is relevant to every society and to every age, while the particulars depend on the relative social setting of a given time and place.

What has been described here is the way Mathews functioned as an exegete asking about the basic foundations and contemporary relevance of the social teachings of Jesus. However, Mathews as a constructive theologian does see the attitudes and acts inspired by the love ideal represented in the person of the historical Jesus as the motive force of an evolutionary movement toward the attainment of a kingdom of universal justice and fraternity in the present age. Hence, while in *The Social Teachings of Jesus* (1897) Mathews believed that Jesus understood the kingdom as an ideal social order to be gradually realized on earth, he now interprets Jesus as an apocalypticist but retains for himself

the goal of a progressively attained divine brotherhood which he formerly attributed also to Jesus. If
men pattern their lives after the love ideal embodied
in Jesus' precept and example, a better social order
will result. Mathews continued to believe until the
end of his life that the ideals of Jesus would more
and more come to prevail among men.

In short, we discover in Shailer Mathews a splendid example of the liberal quest of the historical
Jesus within the framework of "the Chicago School"
—the most outstanding effort yet seen to forge a
distinctively American tradition in biblical interpretation and theological reconstruction. The combination of the task of reconstructing the past as it
really was (history) with a dynamic-organic model
of society (sociology) led to the development of the
socio-historical method. Mathews used this method
both to gain an understanding of the Christian tradition and to work out a contemporary reconstruction
of the ancient gospel. The key assumption running
throughout his work is the notion of Christianity
as a religious-social movement which reproduces in
every new generation an identifiable form of religion
and ethics which is given intellectual legitimization
by an interpretation of the faith and experience of
believers in terms which are organically related to
the prevailing social mind. True to his liberal orientation, he looked to the man Jesus of Nazareth as
the source and norm of experiences which constitute
Christian existence as a definable entity in every
age. His confidence in the socio-historical method
and his liberal theological perspective combined to
assure him that the quest of the historical Jesus was

both historically possible and theologically legitimate.[53] Led by his historical studies to the conclusions that Jesus was a proponent of apocalypticism,
he found it necessary to distinguish between the
absolute, timeless elements of the gospel of the kingdom which were based on the character and will of
God and the relativistic, ephemeral aspects of the
New Testament framework. In this way he was able,
to his own satisfaction, to separate nut from shell
and hence to work out his own kind of "demythologizing program." To borrow Harry Emerson
Fosdick's terminology, the "abiding experiences"
of a God who loves and demands love have been and
must be interpreted in the "changing categories"
provided by some contemporary sociocultural mentality. Sacrificial social-mindedness or the outgoing
goodwill exemplified in Jesus of Nazareth is the
norm of the regenerated life, and dedication to the
timeless love-ideal leads toward the coming of a
universal brotherhood among men under the father-
hood of God. It is within this framework that the
detailed social teachings of Jesus are to be understood. We cannot reproduce the specifics of his own
views, for they are bound to a time and place far
removed. But his insights into the human condition
overarch the centuries and call for incarnation into
the stuff of today's world. The abiding legacy of
Jesus, then, is his call to men to unify their moral
lives around the confidence that they are spiritual
beings who transcend economic-material, physio-

[53] The terminology is taken from James M. Robinson's *A New Quest
of the Historical Jesus* (London: SCM, 1959), in reference to critics
who have argued that the "old quest" as represented by Mathews is
both "historically impossible" and "theologically illegitimate." See
pp. 26–47.

chemical forces and for whom neighbor-directed sacrificial goodwill is the most practical human ideal.

EVALUATION

How shall we measure the enduring worth of Mathews's proposals? In the first place, as has already been indicated, the apocalyptical view of the kingdom of God to which Mathews was converted soon after the turn of the century has been sustained by subsequent scholarship. Moreover, his attempt to distinguish between the eschatological setting of the moral imperatives of Jesus and their ultimate grounding in the character and will of God coincides with efforts among numerous later scholars. By this stratagem Mathews was enabled to call attention to elements of historical relativity in Jesus' proclamation without giving up the claim to the abiding validity of his basic ethical themes. Hence, he was never tempted to take the path followed by Albert Schweitzer in designating the teachings of Jesus as an "interim ethic" now rendered obsolete by the nonoccurrence of the expected end of history. With regard to other major issues such as the certainty with which the real Jesus of history may be discovered by critical research and the relationship of the message of Jesus to the kerygma of the early church, basic new directions have emerged to which attention needs to be directed briefly.

The main line of New Testament scholarship has passed through at least two major phases since the period of the liberal quest to which Mathews belongs. First of all, there was a serious reassessment of the nineteenth-century effort to discover the man Jesus behind the dogmas of the church through means of objective historical investigation. This story of this search for Jesus as he really was has been thoroughly documented in Schweitzer's famous work, *The Quest of the Historical Jesus.* This book marks, though it did not cause, the end of the period it describes. The quest of the Jesus of history was widely abandoned because it was believed to be, in Robinson's now familiar phrase, both "historically impossible and theologically illegitimate."[54] It was historically impossible in that the Gospels do not provide the kind of data that are required to produce a factual biography. The synoptic authors were basically writing as theologians proclaiming the faith of the church and not as documentarians of the life of a famous man. William Wrede[55] and Julius Wellhausen[56] demonstrated this point, while K. L. Schmidt[57] argued persuasively that Mark arranged his material not in chronological order but on the basis of other principles. The form critics showed the Gospels to be made up of independent units previously transmitted orally and shaped to meet the practical needs of the emerging church.[58] Hence, it became more and more difficult to sustain the hope that historians can reconstruct the life of Jesus using materials that were basically designed to serve the theological and practical needs of the Christian

[54] Ibid.

[55] William Wrede, *Das Messiasgeheimnis in den Evangelien* (Göttingen: Vandenhoeck & Ruprecht, 1901).

[56] Julius Wellhausen, *Einleitung in die drei ersten Evangelien* (1906).

[57] K. L. Schmidt, *Der Rahmen der Geschichte Jesu* (1919).

[58] For example, Martin Dibelius, *Die Formgeschichte des Evangeliums* (1919); English translation, *From Tradition to Gospel* (New York: Scribner's, 1934), and Rudolf Bultmann, *Die Geschichte der synoptischen Tradition* (1921); English translation, *The History of the Synoptic Tradition* (New York: Harper, 1963).

community, since it is exceedingly difficult if not
impossible to separate or recover the original words
and deeds of Jesus from traditions and interpretations of the church.[59]

Closely related to the historical question was the
growing claim that the heart of the New Testament
is not the earthly Jesus but the exalted Christ. The
Gospels do not set forth for their own sake the sayings and doings of the human prophet from Nazareth but focus rather on the saving act of God in
the divine Savior and Lord. Not the historical Jesus
known through critical research but the risen Christ
proclaimed in the preaching of the Apostles and
received by faith—this is the content of the New
Testament witness. The discovery of the kerygma
as the center of the Gospels provided the theological
rationale for the alleged illegitimacy of the nineteenth-century quest. Moreover, it shifted the attention of historians from the presentation of objective
facts in chronological order and in their proper
causal relationships to the recovery of the religious
meanings grasped by selves in encounter with the
sacred events of the past. This new approach to the
Gospels and to historical methodology was heralded
in Martin Kahler's epoch-making essay *Der sogen-
annte historische Jesus und der biblische, geschicht-
liche Christus* (1892)[60] and was given repeated

[59] On the other hand, Joachim Jeremias has undertaken to use form
criticism in precisely the opposite direction. By isolating the tendencies
of the church's use of the parable tradition, he attempted to recover
their original form and wording. See his *The Parables of Jesus*, trans.
S. H. Hooke from the 6th ed. of 1962 (New York: Scribner's, 1963),
esp. chap. 2. See also his *The Problem of the Historical Jesus*, trans.
Norman Perrin, Facet Books (Philadelphia: Fortress, 1964), p. 16.

[60] Martin Kahler, *The So-called Historical Jesus and the Biblical,
Historic Christ,* trans. Carl E. Braaten (Philadelphia: Fortress, 1964).

theological reinforcement in the works of the dialec-
tical theologians, among them Karl Barth, Emil
Brunner, and Paul Tillich. The central figure in this
period, however, was Rudolf Bultmann, functioning
both as a New Testament historian and as a theological exponent of the program of demythologizing.[61]
While the rejection of the search for the Jesus of
history has been more characteristic of Continental
than of Anglo-Saxon scholarship, American studies
were also affected, although generally speaking, not
as radically.[62]

A second major development in New Testament
scholarship since Mathews's time consists in the
emergence of a new quest of the man Jesus.[63] This
movement too originated among German scholars
and has been most vigorously pursued by them,
although some Americans have also been prominent
in developing its themes. The new quest was initi-
ated in 1953 by Ernst Käsemann in his lecture on
"The Problem of the Historical Jesus."[64] Subsequent contributions have been made by Ernst Fuchs,
Günther Bornkamm, Gerhard Ebeling, and Hans

[61] See, for example, his *Jesus* (1926) ; English translation, *Jesus and
the Word* (New York: Scribner paperback, 1958), "New Testament
and Mythology," *Kerygma and Myth*, ed. Hans Werner Bartsch (New
York: Harper Torchbook, 1961), pp. 1–44. This last article stating his
famous demythologizing proposal was published in Germany in 1941.

[62] See Roy Harrisville, "Representative American Lives of Jesus,"
The Historical Jesus and the Kerygmatic Christ, ed. Carl Braaten and
Roy Harrisville (New York: Abingdon, 1964), pp. 172–196. Cf. also
Robinson, *New Quest*, p. 9, where he speaks of the relatively uninter-
rupted quest going on in French and Anglo-Saxon circles.

[63] A standard treatment is Robinson, *New Quest*. See also Reginald
H. Fuller, *The New Testament in Current Study* (New York: Scribner's,
1962), pp. 25–53.

[64] Käsemann's essay is now available in *Essays on New Testament
Themes*, Studies in Biblical Theology 41 (Naperville: Allenson, 1964).

Conzelmann, on the Continent, and by James Robinson in this country. A major concern of these men has been the fear that the concentration on the kerygmatic Christ might result in a mythological construct of faith unrelated to the message and ministry of the man Jesus who really lived and died. Their aim is to show that the mythological categories employed by the church in its proclamation of the Christ—preexistence, virgin birth, the atonement, the resurrection, and exaltation—were authentic interpretations of the person, the preaching, the intentions, and the deeds of the real man Jesus of Nazareth. The basic issue concerns the continuity between the preaching of Jesus and the proclamation of the church, between the earthly Jesus and the exalted Christ. If we are not to fall into a kind of kerygma docetism, it is theologically important, even necessary, to demonstrate this continuity.

But not only is it theologically required, it is historically possible to conduct a new quest. The justification of this claim, as developed by Robinson, is basically twofold. In the first place, an understanding of historiography is required which looks not to objective, external facts properly ordered but to the intentions and commitments of persons expressed in their words and deeds. Selfhood resides in and is constituted by such intentions and commitments. Moreover, the kerygmatic interests of the early church would naturally lead to the preservation of the very materials from the life of Jesus which would provide the clues required for the understanding of his selfhood. In short, the church remembered those words and deeds of Jesus which most authentically expressed his aims and motives, his basic message and goals. Moreover, form criticism itself has developed criteria which make it possible with considerable success to trace traditions back to their original basis in the life setting of Jesus himself (see nn. 58 and 59). Hence, a new historiography involving a new understanding of selfhood combined with careful analysis of the materials preserved in the kerygmatic witness of the Gospels does make it possible to recover the real Jesus of history, that is, the authentic selfhood residing in his intentions and commitments. Modern historical research can provide a second access to Jesus alongside the apostolic witness to him which is sufficient to make possible a test as to whether there is indeed a continuity between the fundamental message and mission of the historical Jesus and the existential content of the kerygmatic witness to the exalted Lord and Christ. Not surprisingly the new questers give a positive answer in every case.

It cannot be said that the basic questions concerning the historical object of Christian faith have been brought to any final resolution by this recent movement in New Testament studies. On the contrary, the new quest has already been subjected to searching criticism, and old questions continue to be debated with vigor but with no end in sight.[65] At a minimum, however, it can be said that the confidence with which Mathews and other members of the

[65] In addition to the books by Robinson and Fuller, an introduction to the issues under current discussion may be found in two books edited by Roy Harrisville and Carl Braaten, *Kerygma and History* (New York: Abingdon, 1962), and *The Historical Jesus and the Kerygmatic Christ*. In this latter volume see the articles by Braaten and one by Ogden and Harvey for vigorous criticisms of the new quest. A good discussion of the methodological issues involved may be found in Van Harvey, *The Historian and the Believer* (New York: Macmillan, 1966).

Chicago School approached the issue was much too premature. The socio-historical method does not provide once and for all an access to Jesus which renders theological debate about his status as the Christ any less necessary or complex. But neither have the successive movements in New Testament scholarship brought us much closer to a settlement of the basic issues. Apparently each generation must think out for itself the meaning of Jesus as the Christ in the light of the historical tools and theological resources available to it.[66] Hence, while we cannot rest content with Mathews's own approach to the quest of the historical Jesus, neither can we judge him from some superior vantage point enabling us to mark out with precision the exact mixture of truth and error in his writings.

Brief notice should be taken of the fact that Mathews did not focus exclusively on the man Jesus as the sole legitimate object of Christian faith. There is another trend represented in *Atonement and the Social Process*. Here he deals with the various theological interpretations given in the New Testament and in Christian history to the role of Jesus as the atoning Christ who mediates the forgiveness of God to sinners. From this perspective Jesus is viewed as the divinely sent Savior who does whatever is necessary to make the mercy of God available to repentant hearts. The requirements differ in every age, so that doctrines of atonement are relative to time and place. But what is constant is the formal model of Jesus functioning as the reconciling Christ. In Mathews's own reconstruction Jesus is said to be

[66] I have stated my own views in *Science, Secularization, and God* (New York: Abingdon, 1969), pp. 195–221.

the source and norm of cosmic adjustment, i.e., a right relationship between men and their total environment. In short, both in his historical analysis and in his own theological interpretation Mathews recognizes that theology is not concerned exclusively with the life, personality, and teachings of Jesus the man as such, but that it has seen and should see him in his paradigmatic role of the saving Lord, the mediator of divine forgiveness, and the guide to fulfillment. There are obvious similarities in this side of Mathews's thought to the kerygmatic theology of the recent generation with its distinction between the factual, historical Jesus of history and the interpreted, biblical Christ.

CONCLUSION

Every attempt to interpret the Christian message to a particular cultural situation incorporates elements that at best have no lasting significance and at worst require correction by subsequent generations. This judgment applies to the great classical theologians of the past—Augustine, Aquinas, Calvin, and Scheiermacher, for example—and it holds for Shailer Mathews as well. To make this point, however, is to repeat what Mathews himself vigorously contended for. Insistence on the necessity of distinguishing between the permanent, universal values of the Christian religion and the secondary cultural framework in which it is expressed has become commonplace. Mathews should be remembered with gratitude for the careful historical work and critical theological analysis he did in support of this thesis. On this point his neoorthodox successors could only agree. However, they found him

guilty of obscuring the infinite majesty and transcendence of the Holy One of Israel and of under-
playing the truth that man is a rebellious sinner,
freely but inevitably corrupting the divine image by
his universal unrighteousness. Even today Mathews
sounds sentimental to most of us, too optimistic
about the future, too little in anguish over the moral
ambiguities of history and the perfidy of man. Yet
even here we can recognize in him a legitimate note
that focuses on the possibilities that lie ahead as the
fulfillment of the promise and purpose of God. His
was a theology of hope. Many of us believe that an
organic-evolutionary, process-oriented perspective
that focuses on the intention of a loving God to
create and bring to maturity a community of loving
persons is the most appropriate form of Christian
theological expression in the present moment.[67] To
develop such a theology is to work in the spirit and
shadow of Shailer Mathews.

[67] My own theology takes this form. See foregoing note.

SELECTED BIBLIOGRAPHY

A. WORKS BY MATHEWS
  1. Books (listed in order of publication)
    The Social Teachings of Jesus. New York: The Macmillan Co., 1897.
    A History of New Testament Times in Palestine. New York: The Macmillan Co., 1899.
    The Messianic Hope in the New Testament. Chicago: The University of Chicago Press, 1905.
    The Social Gospel. Philadelphia: The Griffith & Roland Press, 1910.
    The Gospel and Modern Man. New York: The Macmillan Co., 1910.
    The Spiritual Interpretation of History. Cambridge: The Harvard University Press, 1916.
    The Faith of Modernism. New York: The Macmillan Co., 1924.
    Atonement and the Social Process. New York: The Macmillan Co., 1930.
    The Growth of the Idea of God. New York: The Macmillan Co., 1931.
    New Faith for Old: An Autobiography. New York: The Macmillan Co., 1936.

  2. Articles
    "Theology and the Social Mind," *The Biblical World* 46 (October, 1915): 201–248.
    "Theology as Group Belief," *Contemporary American Theology,* ed. Vergilius Ferm. Manhasset, N. Y.: Round Table Press, 1933, vol. 2, pp. 161–193.

B. INTERPRETATIONS OF MATHEWS

Arnold, Charles Harvey. *Near the Edge of the ·Battle* (Divinity School Association, University of Chicago, 1966), esp. pp. 35–42.

Aubrey, Edwin E. "Theology and the Social Process," *The Process of Religion*, ed. Miles Krumbine. New York: The Macmillan Co., 1933, pp. 17–52.

Cauthen, Kenneth. *The Impact of American Religious Liberalism*. New York: Harper, 1962, Chapter 8.

Smith, Kenneth L. "Shailer Mathews: Theologian of Social Process." Ph.D. diss., Duke University, 1959.

JESUS ON
SOCIAL INSTITUTIONS

PREFACE BY THE AUTHOR

Interest in the social implications of the Christian religion has greatly broadened since 1895, when I began the publication of a series of articles on Christian Sociology in the "American Journal of Sociology." These articles, after changes, were published as *The Social Teaching of Jesus* in 1897. Although Free-mantle, Westcott, Abbott, Strong, Ely, Herron, Hill, and Gladden had aroused the conscience of the church to its social obligations, so far as I know this volume was the first attempt in America to study systematically and exegetically the bearing of the gospel material upon social institutions. The interest in the subject was extended by the notable works of Peabody, Rauschenbusch, Vedder, and Ward. At the same time social science was rapidly developing and the place of religion among social forces and controls was being more sharply defined in a considerable literature, both sociological and psychological. As important as these two types of studies was the application of historical methods to the study of the New Testament in order to appreciate the social and religious forces which affected its authors and the early stages of the Christian movement.

The field in which these various investigations overlapped has become one of special significance because of its bearing upon the interpretation of Jesus and the meaning of his work. My interest in the subject led to the publication of a number of volumes, among them

The Church and the Changing Order, The Messianic Hope in the New Testament, The History of New Testament Times in Palestine, and, with Professor E. D. Burton, *The Life of Christ.* It was, however, the study of the revolutionary spirit, in preparation for my volume, *The French Revolution, 1789-1815,* that particularly convinced me of the bearing of social psychology upon the study of Jesus as a factor in the development of civilization. This little book is the outcome of this conviction. It replaces my *Social Teaching of Jesus,* although I have not hesitated to use some portions of this older work.

S. M.

I.

THE REVOLUTIONARY SPIRIT IN THE
TIME OF JESUS

IN the year 27—or was it 29?—of the era to which he was to give his name, a carpenter, just entering full maturity, closed the door of his shop in Nazareth and stepped into history. Two hundred years later men were to believe that he was the incarnation of God born without earthly father. In a thousand years they were to regard him as the God-man who by his death made it possible for God to forgive those whom he selected from a rebellious and lost humanity. In less than two thousand years he had been worshiped by thousands of millions of men and women who believed that they had miraculously drunk of his blood and partaken of his flesh. But of all this none of his friends and acquaintances in Nazareth had any thought. To them Jesus was a carpenter, the son of a carpenter; a member of a rather large family, none of whom had given any indication of exceptional ability.

Jesus was born in one of the great moments of history. A few years before his birth a young man without title had seized the political institutions of the Roman Republic, had gradually accumulated power which made him master of legislation and head of the army in a vast state. About the time when, as a boy, Jesus visited Jerusalem with his father and mother, an old man of seventy was passing laws against bachelors and calling upon his general to give him back the legions lost in the Teutoburg Forest. When he was a man of twenty, the young Germanicus, after establishing the Roman power on the left bank of the Rhine, had died not far from Nazareth, poisoned by a rival. When he was thirty, a Roman Emperor had disarmed the ancient kingdoms of the East and had established a peace that continued for centuries, marred only by political revolts of professional soldiers. For the first time in history an age of commerce and culture sprang into existence. The little strip of land, halfway across which Jesus lived, and over which for millennia armies had marched to defeat or victory, had become the channel through which the Far East poured its commerce and gold into the West.

To all this transformation Jesus was apparently indifferent. While a new world was in the making he was an unnoticed carpenter in a small town without history and without traditions. Yet his abiding significance was to be determined by these changes.* As a Jew he shared in conditions set by the new epoch. For, without leading revolt, he was to live and teach in the atmosphere of revolution, use the language of revolution, make the revolutionary spirit the instrument of his message, and organize a movement composed of men who awaited a divinely given new age.

From such activities sprang Christendom.

I

Jesus and his words must be understood in accordance with historical relativity. Teachings directed to conditions which have been outgrown may not be applied directly to others, but the principles which such specific teachings expressed are his message to a world of which he never dreamed.

To discover these principles one must not look for "historical backgrounds." The approach to a true understanding of Jesus is through social psychology, and particularly through the messianic hope of his people. And the messianic hope is a phase of the psychology of revolution. To understand it one should be a student of revolutions.[1] Now all revolutions are preceded by and spring from the same social attitudes. A new class consciousness is evoked by a sense of political, economic, and social inequality; propaganda arouses a spirit of revolt; a sense of injustice breeds the desire for revenge; an enthusiasm for some abstract ideal provokes a series of outbreaks that attempt to realize the hopes and avenge the wrongs of an oppressed group. A social order with such psychology enters upon actual revolution as it overcomes existing authority. If the privileged classes control a government strong enough to maintain itself against outbreak, revolt is crushed and the fermenting yeast of a revolutionary minority, if not destroyed, is again hidden. If the government shows weakness either by ill-granted concessions or inability to put down disorders, radical change in political and social conditions will follow.

The history of Judea for more than the century and a half beginning with the days of Herod I is an illustration of the former of these pre-revolutionary situations, just as France in the eighteenth century is an illustration of the second. Rome crushed the revolutionary movements in Palestine; the Bourbons and the

[1] See Mathews, *French Revolution, 1789-1815,* pp. 75sq.; LeBon, *Psychology of Revolution;* Lombroso, *La Crime politique et la Révolution;* Edwards, *The Natural History of Revolution.*

old régime were crushed by the French middle class. But the approach to all revolutions is through a study of a conditioning psychology.

II

Jesus lived in a glorious and creative period. Rome had looted the East and inaugurated a period of feverish commercial development never reached before. For the only time in history Western civilization was not military. The Empire evolving from the Republic included in itself practically all of Europe south of the Rhine and the Danube, and all Asia and Africa that once constituted the Arabian and Turkish Empires. For the only time in history the vast territory enjoyed a single administration. As social orders go, it was sane and wholesome. Nations that had for centuries been engaged in war had turned themselves to commerce, art, literature, and the amenities of a genuine civilization. To a considerable extent there was local self-government, although national codes had been modified in the interest of a superimposed Roman system which had crushed any attempt at nationality. One nation alone refused to be repressed.

The little tetrarchy of Galilee and the little procuratorial province of Judea were on no distant frontier, but in the center of the political history of this vast Empire. Whereas Gaul was newly emerging from the condition described by Caesar, the eastern lands of the Mediterranean possessed the most highly developed civilization of the times. It was there that the fate of the Empire and Western civilization had been settled. For a hundred years there was hardly a great Roman who was not made or broken at the eastern end of the Mediterranean. Caesar, Pompey, Crassus,

Anthony, and Augustus had all there fought decisive battles.

History has moved westward in these later days, and the Near East has become an international liability, but in the days of Jesus it was still prosperous. The coast cities from Jaffa to Antioch were alive with commerce. Around the little Sea of Galilee there were nine cities of considerable size. Galilee, no larger than many an American county, was said to have over two hundred villages and small towns, as well as four walled cities. The ancient Holy Land had ceased to be a land of a single people. Its Greek population was as numerous as the Jewish, and the traveler stands in amazement before the ruins of noble cities in what is now all but a wilderness. Everywhere the efficiency of Rome was in evidence. Order had been forced upon Palestine as upon other states.

The Jews were no more oppressed than other nations, and in fact were granted a number of special privileges which Josephus describes at length.[2] Their prejudices were respected. They were given full religious privileges and were not forced to sacrifice to the genius of the Republic. With the exception of Judea and Samaria they were under native rulers. Their cities were being rebuilt, disorders of all sorts were effectively put down, and they were enjoying a prosperity which they had never known before.

But while other nations coerced into prosperity accepted the control of Rome submissively, the Jews grew restive. In this they were not unique. India objects to the efficiency of British rule; Korea chafes under the prosperity brought by Japan; the Philip-

[2] Mathews, *New Testament Times in Palestine*, 141*sq.* Various decrees favoring the Jews are given by Josephus, *Ant.* xiii, 9:2; xiv, 8:5; xiv, 10; xiv, 12; xvi, 6; xix, 5; xx, 1:2.

pines seek independence from the American control which has established schools and order. Indeed, most nations which have never exercised strong self-government become restless and often revolutionary when given order and prosperity by some efficient conqueror. Enjoying blessings which while independent they have not been able to achieve, they long for independence.

This was the psychology of the Jews in Palestine. They looked back more than a millennium to the days of David and Solomon with passionate regret. Their little state, which had then been able to maintain its sovereignty for a few years, was idealized with all the sentiment with which men themselves incapable of achieving great things look upon the deeds of their ancestors. Instead of peace and municipal growth, the Jews could see only the policeman and the soldier. Instead of prosperity, they could see only the tax collector. Instead of freedom of worship, they could see only the Temple guard of Roman soldiers who kept them from religious massacres. Instead of cities like Caesarea, Samaria, Tiberias, and those of the Decapolis, they could see only the standards of the foreign power. Their suppressed nationalism turned to the praise of their past, the glorification of David, and the hope for the reëstablishment of a. Davidic dynasty through the aid of their God. Thus was revolution in the making. The terrible days of 66-70 A. D. and 135 A. D. were its result.

III

Prosperity was not evenly shared by all classes in Palestine. Large sections of the cities were populated by Greeks who were gaining commercial advantages. Among the Jews themselves there was developing a

class whose economic interests were increasingly those
of the controlling non-Jewish population. The Sadducees, although they supplied the high priests, cannot
be understood as merely a group of religionists; nor
were they, like some of their countrymen, mere satel-
lites of the Herods. They represented the conservative
capitalist group, given position by religious privilege,
which refused to share in the theological development
centered about the exposition and codification of Jewish law favored by the lay group of Pharisees. They
clung tenaciously to the older type of Mosaism, regarded the law as binding because of the oath taken in
the days of Ezra, and magnified the class interests of
the priestly families to which they belonged. Like all
those who monopolize economic privileges, they looked
with suspicion upon the new growth of education. To
them the legalistic system which was ultimately to find
codification in the Talmud represented an expanding
idealism which threatened political disturbances.
Their interests, like those of similar classes in every
age, were inseparable from the institutions of the past,
and they preferred the worship of the Temple with
its ritual to the new ethics of the Synagogue with its
insistence upon Jewish exclusiveness. And from the
point of view of social quiet they were wise. Revolution lay in the path of the Pharisee and his policy of
deepening the Jewish spirit.

Over against this relatively small privileged class
were great masses of the people whom the administration was to control and make support the state. The
elaborate city rebuilding demanded income, and income
could come from taxes alone. In a country without
organized industry, taxes must largely take the form of
customs. Even the reduction of taxes under Herod I

had not removed the ubiquitous tax collector, the visible evidence of an alien government. Agriculture, fishing, and trading gave no opportunity for the organization of labor, but every opportunity for the spread of discontent. In the modern sense of the word the proletariat did not exist, but the great mass of the inhabitants of Judea were poor. They crowd the pages of Josephus, poverty stricken, without means of improving their condition. They had little food to eat, little clothing to wear, poor houses in which to live. As in Ireland of a century ago, emigration was the sole escape from the economic pressure which was the price of imperial splendor. It was natural that there should have been a growing hatred of everything that stood for the inequitably distributed prosperity. It was not simply that the masses of the people abhorred Rome and its administration; their hatred extended to those who in any way represented the taxing power.[3] Even the use of the Temple treasures to relieve unemployment failed to placate them.[4] When the great revolt broke out in 66 A.D., the high priest was a victim of mob violence. Archives with their mortgages were among the first objects destroyed.

IV

This spirit of discontent with political subjection and economic inequality expressed itself in preparation for revolution and catastrophe, popularly known as the Messianic Hope.* Religious education, political insurrections, and a cryptic literature were its means.

1. A religious movement is never an end in itself. It springs from needs. Men undertake to organize

[3] Josephus, *Jewish War* ii, 17:2-5.
[4] Josephus, *Ant.* xx, 9:6, 7.

themselves and their religion in such a way as will
bring certain desired ends to pass. Judaism was no
exception to the rule. Within it was a new development of the original movement of Ezra to codify the
customs and institutions which determined the relation
of the Hebrew people with their God. A Utopian
nationalism was in the making. The separation of the
people of Judea from the Samaritans as well as all
pagan people was a primary obligation. The development of the general Mosaic Code into detailed statutes
was intended to develop a sense of national solidarity
and exclusiveness through the worship of Jehovah.
Judaism was not an academic system of religious teaching, but an exposition of the divinely appointed way
by which Jews and Jews alone were to prepare for
national greatness.

One form of this preparation was educational, the
work of the Pharisees.

The Pharisees were the outcome of the nationalistic
movement.[5] They originated in the loyalty to the
national worship of Jehovah which had led to the
uprising under Simon the Maccabee and the Pious.
For a few years under the later Asmoneans they constituted a definite political group within the nation.
After the institution of the Roman control, though
deprived of political significance, their essential character was not changed. They formed a group of non-
priestly, lay associates, insisting upon a rigid ethnic
and religious exclusiveness in every aspect of life. To
this end they set themselves seriously by a detailed
application of the Law to enforce a ceremonial cleanli-

[5] See not only the older discussion in Schürer, *The Jewish People
in the Time of Jesus Christ,* but Herford, *The Pharisees;* Lauterback,
The Sadducees and the Pharisees; Riddle, *Jesus and the Pharisees;*
Jackson and Lake, *The Beginnings of Christianity,* I, 35-136.

ness which opposed contact with anything that was not
Jewish. Although never numbering more than six
thousand members, this association of the "Separated"
became progressively the leaven of an anti-gentile
nationalism. As opposed to the conservatism of the
Sadducees who preferred to restrict religion to the worship of the Temple, the Pharisee sought to develop in
the synagogues an intense Judaism utterly distinct
from the life of any other nation. The hostility
between the two groups was thus more than that difference in doctrine of which Josephus [6] speaks. Such
differences were not wanting, but beneath them
dominant social attitudes were found.[*]

The purpose of the Pharisaic movement cannot be
found in mere interest in academic discussion or hyper-
conscientiousness or even religious universalism. Such
elements were present, but back of the acute and
elaborate discussion of the scholars of Judaism is to be
seen a psychology bent on applying the Law—both
written and traditional—to the Jewish religious life,
so that the nation might be judged by its God to be
worthy of the empire of the world. The Pharisees even
sought to establish a universal religion by the conver-
sion of the Gentiles to Judaism. To this end they
expanded educational ideals and methods through the
synagogue. This in itself was not to favor revolution,
but it furthered a revolutionary complex by its development of a national class consciousness, a sense of
injustice, a hope for supremacy, and a centering of
attention upon customs and regulations which prepared a people and its non-Jewish adherents for the
divine overthrow of enemies. From this point of view
it is easy to see why the rank and file of people were

[6] *Ant.* xviii, 1:3-5; *War* ii, 8:2-14.

under their influence.[7]   Doubtless they made the
appeal which so frequently attends any claim of
intellectual superiority, but there was something deeper
than this. The ignorant *am-ha-aretz,* the masses, who
did not know the law, could not keep it. Thus unwittingly and unintentionally they were holding back the
day of deliverance. Yet only as the whole nation could
keep the law could the divine interposition be expected.[8]
Therefore the Pharisees turned, though without much
hope, to the extension of a knowledge of the Law
among the masses.

The political bearing of such a religious complex is
obvious. Whatever may have been the Pharisees'
thoughts of the life after death, all individual motives
for righteousness were supplemented if not submerged
in the belief that members of a nation must be holy if
the nation were to be the master of the world.[9] Such
a mastery was quite impossible unless God miraculously granted his assistance and leadership. But such
divine interposition would be impossible until the
nation itself kept the Law, the outstanding evidence of
God's favor.*

2. The second form taken by the revolutionary
nationalism was that of insurrection. The records of
the time abound in tales of abortive uprisings as one
generation after another produced leaders or groups
who sought to "tread on the neck of the eagle." These
revolts had been speedily and terribly crushed by the
Roman administrators of Palestine, but they were to
continue for a generation after the time of Jesus until

[7] Josephus, *Ant.* xiii, 10:5, 6.
[8] Moore, *Judaism,* I, 282; II, 72, 158, mentions this, but only
incidentally.
[9] See, for instance, Psalms of Solomon, 1:5-9; 2:3, 5, 8; 4:5; 7:2,
8:9-14.

the later Roman procurators proved incapable of repressing them, and the whole land blazed into civil war which lasted from 66 to 70 A.D. and was stamped out only by Titus himself. And even this repression was temporary. It was not until 135 A.D. that the Jewish nationalism was finally extirpated in the tragedy that brought about the death of the great Rabbi Akiba, who had thrown in his lot with Bar Kozibar, whom he hailed as the expected Deliverer.*

Josephus [10] in accounting for the outbreak of 66 A.D. declares: "What most stirred them up to the war was an ambiguous oracle which was found also in their sacred writings, that about that time one from their country should become ruler of the world." Doubtless the reference here is to the Book of Daniel, which at that time seemed to have a wide circulation. Josephus describes also a movement apparently among the younger Jews during the troubled times which followed the banishment of Archelaus in 6 A.D. The leaders were a Judas of Gamala, a Galilean, and a Pharisee named Zaduk. Josephus, in describing this movement, says: "Its disciples agree in all other things with the Pharisaic notions but they have an inviolable attachment to liberty, and say that God is their only ruler and Lord." [11] Only the existence of a widespread feeling of revolutionary discontent could account for the repeated appearance of "prophets" and outlaws who could, like Theudas a few years after Christ, lead a great company into the wilderness in the expectation of miracles, or like the Egyptian who promised his followers that he would stand on the Mount of Olives and cause the walls of Jerusalem to fall.[12] That the people were subject to propaganda also appears from

[10] *War* vi, 5, 4.
[11] *Ant.* xviii, 1, 6.
[12] *Ant.* xx, 8, 6; *War* ii, 13, 5; cf. Acts 21:38.

THE REVOLUTIONARY SPIRIT 23

the obscure words of Josephus,[13] in which he speaks
of a "body of wicked men cleaner in their hands but
more wicked in their intentions, who destroyed the
peace of the city no less than did these murderers (the
Sicarii), for they were for innovations and changes."

This instability of the popular mind, this readiness of
the masses to gather about some leader, are plain on
the pages of the New Testament, and undoubtedly
constituted a real danger in the minds of the government and the privileged classes. In fact it lay beneath
the formal charge brought by the members of the
Sanhedrin against Jesus as one "perverting the nation
and forbidding to pay tribute to Caesar, saying that he
himself is Christ a king," and as "stirring the people,
teaching throughout all Judea, beginning from Galilee
to this place." [14]

All of these facts point in the same direction, namely,
a revolutionary attitude of a large portion of society,
a sensitiveness to political and economic inferiority, a
hope of deliverance which would make the Jews the
rulers of the world, a fusing of these expectations with
the faith that God would empower the nation by
miraculous leadership and strength to accomplish the
revolution and the conquest which should make their
and his kingdom possible. The leader, himself empowered for his task by the spirit of God, was known as the
Messiah—the "Anointed."

Nothing is more unpalatable to the revolutionary
mind than administrative details. It wants absolute,
abstract ideals. When these ideals represent a condition believed to have been lost, their emotional appeal
is tremendous. Discontented masses are not swayed
by programs of administration, but by the promised

[13] *War* ii, 13, 4.
[14] Luke 23:2-5.

resurrection of lost privileges. The social philosophers of the eighteenth century found it in the natural man and natural rights. The *Social Compact*, anything but a codification of tribal customs, set forth an ideal which stirred men to replevin rights wrongly enjoyed by kings and nobles. The Marxian socialist sees in capital loot taken from and to be retaken by the laborer. The Jew's hope was that of a new nation given imperial control over a conquered world through the aid of the God of Abraham.[15]

3. This hope had its literature. The so-called apocalypses are its code language. They undertook to comfort a nation in distress by setting forth the coming triumph of the nation in the language of visions. This apocalyptic literature was deeply religious, but in outlook it was political rather than theological. There is no little discussion as to whether the apocalypses represented the abnormal experience of the writers, but such a view is less tenable than that the apocalypse is a literary form in which the revolutionary spirit could express itself without danger of punishment. Detached from the psychology of the nation, this literature has been interpreted as if it represented a new form of the Jewish religion. This is a mistake. It was the code language of the revolutionary spirit. The literature of prerevolutionary epochs is frequently cryptic. Visions with their symbols are a familiar literary device, and apocalyptic literature from the days of Daniel to the revolution in Ireland is no exception to the general rule. It is an attempt to express and incite the revolutionary spirit by the appeal to religion or its substitute.

The empire to be established as the kingdom of God

---

[15] It is this picture of expected glories that Edwards, *Natural History of Revolution*, calls "the revolutionary myth."

was not heaven, but a kingdom of Jews on the earth. Yet the apocalyptic pictures of its triumph break across politics into supernaturalism. Jewish hopes were not based merely upon the processes of social revolution, but upon the actual power of God. Here supernaturalism reached still further into history. The kingdom of God, that is to say, the social order in which his will was perfectly done, was still in heaven where angels were its perfect subjects. Yet even in heaven there had been revolt, from which had come a second superhuman kingdom, that of Satan. As God wished to do people good and establish righteousness, so Satan wished to do people harm and establish wickedness. Thus a dualism emerged which was not philosophical. With no other patterns for his thought than those given by his political experience, the Jew turned for material for his theological thinking, not to cosmology but to politics. History became a struggle between two rival superhuman beings. With the evil being or Satan were allied the fallen angels and the earthly enemies of Judaism. With God were the Jews.

Only one empowered by God could be trusted to vanquish oppressors and the supernatural powers behind them. This interplay of transcendental and political conceptions appeared in the outcome which the Jew expected. There was to be cosmic struggle between God and Satan as well as between God and Romans, and the final outcome was to be a new heaven and a new earth in which the Jewish nation under the leadership of the Messiah was to be supreme over a crushed and bleeding world.

Naturally such a literary medium tended to the bizarre and illogical. Unrestrained by the decorum of literal expressions, committed to supernaturalism, the seer permitted his mind not only to revel in images, but also in situations which themselves were symbolic. If patriots were to be thought of as sheep and oppressors as birds of prey, it was not difficult to believe that the author of the visions had mounted to heaven under the conduct of an angel. If the glories of the ancient nation were to be revived and the hated political masters massacred, the apocalyptist felt free to see the individual Jews brought back from the dead to share in the new nation. He could picture an abyss of burning fire for the giants and devils and bad people and Romans. All reserves set by a sense of reality were abandoned, and the apocalyptist surrendered himself to the intoxicating hope of a heavenly deliverance and a heavenly Deliverer.

It is possible to abstract from this literature a tolerably consistent view of the future,[16] and if one is indifferent to the actual psychology from which the literature sprang, it is not difficult to find in it non-political expectations of the future which may well give rise to doubts as to the writer's sanity. But there is no evidence that even in their wildest pictures of coming glory the Jews looked forward to anything fundamentally different from the sort of life which they were then living.[17] Certainly they were not swayed by the Hellenistic views of heaven and hell which were subsequently appropriated by the Christians and used to give content to biblical expressions. Insofar as religion can be discovered in the apocalyptic system, it is a political hope involving supernatural and all but super-rational elements. Even though the Davidic Prince is less in evidence in the later apocalyptic liter-

[16] Mathews, *The Messianic Hope in the New Testament*, pt. i; Charles, *Eschatology* (1899), chs. v-viii, esp. pp. 299-305.
[17] See, for instance, Enoch 10:10-17.

ature,[18] to erect apocalyptism into an independent religious conception and to speak of its eschatology as if it were something akin to the modern premillennialism, is to read back into Jewish hopes ideas which were impossible until strictly nationalist hopes had been abandoned. The apocalyptic literature, like the religious nationalism of the Pharisee and the direct action of the Zealots and "robbers," was an expression of a revolutionary psychology. The cause of a people was the cause of God, its enemies were supported by Satan, and the coming triumph of Jewish institutions was to be due to divine assistance of a holy nation in a war that a Messiah should lead through massacre to victory. For this great day Pharisee and rebel alike sought to prepare the nation.

To a mind dominated by syllogistic consistency, such a complex of war, politics, religion, cosmology, Persian dualism, and religious symbolism seems so logically inconsistent as to be incredible. The Greek had his eschatological pictures of heaven and hell, his philosophy and his mythology, his politics and his Golden Age, his Necessity and his gods. But he never confused them. Farthest possible was he from feeling that they would unite in the divine establishment of a Greek superstate, among whose inhabitants would be those who had been brought back from Sheol. To the Jew the revolutionary complex was one of dynamic hope colored by the desire for revenge in the name of justice.*

V

It does not aid an understanding of Jesus to abstract a severely scientific and detailed eschatological system

[18] Cf. Case, *Jesus.*

from this psychology. Its really significant elements
are simple: (1) the defeat of Satan by God; (2) the
defeat of the Romans by God's aid given to the Jews;
(3) the complete establishment of the will of God in
the Jewish people by observance of the Mosaic law,
as a preparation for the divinely established Jewish
kingdom; (4) the reliance upon force, violence, and
massacre to bring about this social order.

Obviously with such a conception, God is primarily
interested in enforcing his law and punishing those
who do not keep it. His love is directed toward a
nation and his virtues are those of a sovereign. He is
to be feared rather than loved. His salvation was the
establishment of a Jewish empire. His appointed
Deliverer was to be a conqueror.

But one fact is not to be ignored. No genuinely
revolutionary psychology is pathological. Idealism,
passionate and religious, was in this revolutionary
psychology of messianism. Theology and philosophy
were only incidental. The future was not to perpetuate the present. God was to save. Injustice and irre-
ligion were to end. This is the glory of Judaism.
Beside it the pictures of a past Golden Age with which
contemporary poets of Rome sought to gild the rule
of Augustus seem dilettantism. The religous faith of
the fellow citizens of Jesus was desperately in earnest.
In it lay human values that needed to be reinterpreted
rather than opposed. To accomplish this proved to be
the task and opportunity of Jesus. He taught men
who were already committed to discontent with existing social conditions to have faith in the power of God
to establish a new age. He was a leader of a band of
hope.

II.

JESUS AND THE REVOLUTIONARY SPIRIT

The sympathies of Jesus lay with men swayed by this revolutionary psychology. In time he joined them. He must have been aware of the serious nature of such a step. He must have known how insurrection had risen only to be crushed; how "robbers" had organized short-lived revolutions; how Judas of Gaulanitis and a Pharisee named Zaduk had headed a revolt, "professing an inviolable devotion to liberty, saying that God was their only ruler and lord." None the less he joined a mass movement under the leadership of John, a young man of his own age, who suddenly emerged from the wilderness of Judea as the prophet of the day.

A Nazarite, living on the rudest fare and clothed in the rudest garments, John issued no call to arms, but assumed the rôle of a prophet. Around his birth, as around that of Jesus, were to gather stories of supernatural appearances, but of John himself we have only fragmentary information. Yet upon one thing the traditions of the Christian church and Josephus alike agree. He became the center of a mass movement of those who awaited the new Age. His message was not a call to social transformation, but to preparation for the impending Judgment Day. Men who awaited the interposition of God in national affairs were not to precipitate a revolution. The deliverance would be the act of God himself. Those who would share in

29

its joys were to repent, profess their new hope by sym-
bolical bath, and lead honest and generous lives.

Beginning somewhere in the lower Jordan valley,
John worked his way northward, drawing to himself
crowds of the less privileged. The intelligentsia saw
in him only an object of half-hearted inquiry. When
he told them that he was not the expected leader,* they
apparently had no further concern about him as a
prophet, and he continued northward, throwing back
upon the crowds that followed him their own fears and
hopes. Day after day he sounded the call to preparation by repentance, until, as he reached almost the
frontier of Galilee, the Galileans began to come to him.
Among them were several young men from the towns
on the northern coast of the Sea of Galilee. Presently
Jesus heard of the prophet of the Reign of God and
himself joined the movement. Such an act was expensive. It cost him his occupation, his family, and
ultimately his life. But he had found one who uttered
his own deepest convictions: that the kingdom which
the Jews awaited was not to be born of violence and
acquisitiveness, but was to be God's gift to those who
were prepared to enter it. To him, as to John, the
revolutionary spirit was not to be insurrectionary, but
spiritual.† Living as he did in the midst of a restless
people, eager to revolt, he had neither led nor joined
any revolutionary undertaking, but now, among all the
revolutionary hopes and programs he saw John's as the
expression of reality. He joined it, professing his faith
by baptism.

I

The paucity of information leaves us without any
complete story of the succeeding events, but there has

come down to us a memory of a crisis within his own spirit. Whether because he saw the limitations of John's message, or whether, as was most likely, he experienced one of those measureless transformations in which a man's deepest emotions and faith find unified self-expression, Jesus no sooner had joined the followers of John than he felt himself the superior of John. John had been a prophet of the coming Christ. Jesus felt that he himself was to be that Christ, the one empowered by the resident spirit of God to found his kingdom when the hour for its founding should strike.*

For men detached from social agitation, to whom history is the criticism of documents, such an experience is to be explained rather than shared. But such neutrality forbids safe interpretation. It is one thing to write a treatise on socialism, and quite another to lead a socialist party; it is one thing to judge a historical movement in retrospect, and another to found the movement itself by the sheer power of individuality. Jesus was one of the rare men of destiny to whom the full significance of power came like a burst of thunder. One moment they are what they have been since boyhood, accumulating unconscious sympathies, developing unwittingly potential powers. And then in a moment of emotional crisis all these inner forces find a mission and a significance. Only those who themselves have been swept away by supreme enthusiasm for a new world-order can appreciate such a new self-consciousness. The ordinary man's moment of spiritual rebirth is a rivulet compared with Niagara when set over against the moment when Gautama, under the *bo*-tree, received the enlightenment, Mahomet had his first vision, and Jesus, at his baptism, felt himself to be the Son of God.†

His first duty was the preparation of expectant souls for the coming kingdom.

II

Jesus reshaped the revolutionary hopes in the crucible of his own individuality. No longer was he to be the small-town artisan. He was the prophet of the coming kingdom, the embodiment of its true character, the revealer of the way by which it was to be entered, the organizer and teacher of those expectant souls who sought to enjoy its heaven-born privileges, its Judge and King, the conqueror of Satan.

When John had suffered the fate of prophets, men flocked to Jesus. In him, as in his predecessor, they saw the possible fulfilment of their hopes.

Only the victim of an ill-selected major premise can see in the creative spirits of history the mechanical mixture of contemporary social forces. Personality can never be reached by analysis. In the processes of life the individual is creative and entire, as well as the heir of origins and environment.[1] Superficially, Jesus and John had many resemblances. Both were in large measure the product of the religious and political ferment of their day. Both refused to sanction violence. Both made rigid ethical demands upon those who would enter the expected kingdom. Both were the centers of popular movements. Both fell victims to the fears and resentments of the privileged classes. But religious history was to gather about Jesus. The explanation of this fact lies in the difference between the two personalities. John had not that experience which so clearly set Jesus apart as a sanctifier of the revolutionary spirit of his people.

[1] Mathews, *The Spiritual Interpretation of History*, 111-18, 168 *seq.*

He was content to decrease.* Jesus was to be a Deliverer.[2]

Only a keen mind can join a revolutionary movement and distinguish between its constructive and its dangerous elements. Jesus would have found it much easier to become a "practical" idealist. This has been the office of many men who have contributed to the progress of human welfare, too often at the expense of their own idealism. They have been forced to utilize that acquisitive passion and appeal to that unifying hatred which are so potent in all revolutionary movements. But to the mind of Jesus both the desire to acquire rights and the passion to injure oppressors were dangerous. His teaching started with the revolutionary idealism of his fellows, but it immediately broke with many of their hopes. He might easily have appealed to their sense of injustice and bidden them to go out and seek their rights. When a depressed minority gains mastery it is seldom the party of fraternity and tolerance. But Jesus chose to lay emphasis not upon the acquisition of rights, but upon the attitude which leads men to share rights. To him brotherliness was more than brotherhood.[3]

Similarly he might have attempted to coerce people into a better way of living. It would be difficult to name a more subtle temptation. It dogs the steps of all idealists and too often has turned social saviors into terrorists. But Jesus refused to appeal to force. The spirit of the Lord which had come upon him gave him power to heal the sick, to free the captive and to preach the gospel to the poor.†

1. To appreciate his appeal to the hope for the

[2] The Fourth Gospel in its earlier chapters is an exposition of this difference between John and Jesus.

[3] Dickie, *The Constructive Revolution of Jesus.*

coming of the day of justice, one must start from the
expectation as socialized among his fellow countrymen
already described.   They expected that God would
empower a man by his resident spirit to become the
savior of his people and the founder of his kingdom.
They believed also that this national salvation was to
be accompanied by the defeat of Satan, to whom their
sufferings were ultimately due.   As this Empowered
One, Jesus had to determine his rôle.   If he were to
be more than magician or *mahdi* or fanatic, there was
laid upon him the obligation to disclose to his followers
just what sort of kingdom of God they were to expect.*
He shared in and started with their expectation of
the great transformation.   He endeavored to set forth
the true nature of the divine interposition in history.
The perception of this task explains why during the
first half of his brief public ministry he spoke so frequently about the Kingdom of God and the defeat of
Satan.*   He was not introducing a new conception; he
was giving new content to revolutionary psychology.
To this end he spoke in parables, endeavoring to show
the true nature of the kingdom of God both he
and his hearers expected.   And this he made pellucidly
clear by his central analogy: God was not an emperor
but a father; the reign of God was not so much a
kingdom as a triumph of the goodwill of God in human
affairs.

If we could look at this announcement without our
theological inheritances, its audacity and courage would
appear startling.   Jesus had discovered love as a dominating force in nature and history, and he clung to it
despite the tragedy of his own experience.   The cross

* This is the meaning of his so-called temptation: Matt. 4:1-11;
Lk. 4:1-13.   It might much better be called the choice of a mission.

was to be its symbol. Before it the military and sanguinary methods of the zealots, the socialized hatred of the masses, and the religious nationalism of Pharisaism alike disappeared. If, as he had experienced it, the dominating quality of the will of God is love, then whoever wishes to enjoy its privilege must himself love. That was all the preparation necessary for sharing in the new world-order. If men could only believe it they could move mountains!

Thus by a single change of pattern Jesus transformed the revolutionary hope into a sacrificial socialmindedness. In his mind the perspective of his teaching was fixed. His conception of the kingdom of God as a perfect world-order—now, alas, only in heaven— in which the goodwill of God is supreme did not remove him from the current of his contemporaries' hopes, but it gave new direction to their faith. So long as they believed that the divinely wrought revolution would be a new Jewish empire they could think of God and duty only in patterns of the soldier and the executioner. But if they thought of that great event as the establishment of goodwill, they would think of their relations to God in the patterns of the parent and the child, and of their relations to each other as that of brothers.

2. Like his contemporaries, Jesus believed that the establishment of the kingdom of God as a gift from God would occur before the generation to which he spoke should have passed away.[5] His immediate followers never doubted this. They were sure that

[5] Mk. 9:1 and parallels; Matt. 10:23; Mk. 10:62.* Matt. 24:34 may refer to the destruction of Jerusalem, but not so Matt. 23:36. On this entire matter see Mathews, *The Messianic Hope in the New Testament,* ii; Schweitzer, *The Quest of the Historical Jesus,* xix; J. Weiss, *Die Predigt Jesus vom Reiche Gottes.*

they lived at the end of an historical epoch and that, as Paul said, each day their salvation drew nearer. They did not even expect that they would all die. If the words attributed to Jesus which express this same expectation are really his—and no critical method which would omit them would leave him the extraordinary character he must have been—his teaching was directed to those who thought that the kingdom of God, with its catastrophes and triumphs, was close at hand.

Such a conclusion has given rise to questions as to his mental health.* Indeed, to those who would interpret Jesus from their observation of pathological psychology and who see in him only the sort of man who suffers from delusions of magnificence, his personality must seem neurasthenic.⁶ For any man who to-day believes that the end of the world is immediately at hand and who attempts to construct a morality on that basis seems a victim of mental incapacity. But in all such interpretations of Jesus there lurks the assumption that everybody who believes in the approaching end of the world is not only mentally unbalanced, but incapable of trustworthy moral distinctions. The answer to such a presupposition might possibly be found in the fact that sane and able men have believed in the approaching end of the world and have relentlessly carried on their undertakings under such a conviction. But one must examine Jesus more in detail and study his mental processes in some other way than that of the generalization which characterizes men who are obsessed with interest in mental disease. Certainly, as a man of

⁶ Bundy, *The Psychic Health of Jesus,* gives general criticism of the discussions of this view.

genius he never stepped across the limits of cold
sanity.[7] His mental processes and attitudes are as
distinguishable from those of the fanatic as they are
from those of the modern scientist. Whatever hold the
sense of the immediacy of the Empire of Miracle had
upon him, and however much he appealed to a similar
belief on the part of his followers, such a belief was
not the cause of his teaching that God.is love and that
love is a practicable basis upon which to build human
life. Such convictions do not originate in any belief
in the approach of crisis, but are sharpened by a loss
of the sense of time. I heard once of a young man
who was told that he was the victim of an incurable
disease and that life at best could be but of a few
months' duration. As with most men, a sense of the
approaching sudden end of life aroused the dominant
characteristics of his character. He promptly took
his savings and went on a prolonged spree. In so
doing he was consistent with his suppressed and ill-
regulated true self. With Jesus, though the temptation to appeal to violence was real, and Peter's urging
of current messianic programs he declared was something over which he might stumble;[8] though in the
last tragic hours of his life he told his followers to buy
swords,[9] to none of these impulses did he himself
yield. The effect of his expectation of the approaching end of time was to focus the timeless elements of
faith and purpose. On the one hand, he tried to make
real to the would-be revolutionists who shared in this
belief that the kingdom when it came would be a
divine family full of love. And on the other hand he
persistently taught that love, as the characteristic of

[7] Cf. Murry, *Jesus, Man of Genius;* Ludwig, *The Son of Man.*
[8] Mk. 8:32, 33.
[9] Lk. 22:35-38.

God, was the indispensable characteristic of those who would enjoy his reign. A timeless ideal was set forth as unaffected by time.

A revolutionary psychology always deals with absolutes. Jesus' detailed application of love to social institutions may have been conditioned by his expectation of the speedy coming of the new age—how little evidence there is of this we shall see later—but such a belief was an element in the historical situation which conditioned his activity and his words. He taught love as a timeless attitude to those who believed in such temporalities as war and education in regard for law.

Jesus found in his own experience a censor of the psychology which he shared and to which he appealed. He looked to God as the ultimate basis of all future blessing, and God he knew as a father rather than a king. This conviction, born of the study of the prophets [10] and reënforced by his own experience, prevented his full acceptance of the revolutionary hopes of those who followed him. The defeat of Satan could be shown in cures, but the reign of God was to be established by God himself. Human effort would not bring it in. Ideals need not be adjusted, therefore, to social processes. The passionate desire on the part of the people for a better social order with better institutions and better authority could be analyzed by Jesus because he felt within himself the spirit of the Heavenly Father. All elements in the hopes of his times that were inconsistent with this filial experience he rejected.

He sublimated the social passion of his following. The calm of the philosopher, the careful balance of the investigator, the neutral weighing of evidence, were

[10] Is. 61:1, 2.

not to be his portion. He told men who longed for justice in a new age and expected it to come through the interposition of God by miracle and bloodshed and national supremacy, that God would indeed intervene, but not in the way they expected. In form their hope was justified, but its content was to be repudiated as out of keeping with his own experience of the divine spirit. They were to prepare for the imminent kingdom of God, but their preparation was the possession of a love like that of the Father who would give them the kingdom.[11] It was as if Jesus said to those who hoped for a new social order: You are right in expecting that God will have a part in the development of such an order, but you are wrong in your conception of the method he will adopt in establishing it. You think that the reign of justice and righteousness will come through the road of violence, blood, and war. When it has really come men will realize that God is love and that brotherliness rather than coercion is the true basis for human relations. You think of God as having given laws which can be expanded into minute statutes and that the day of joy and deliverance will come when men keep these statutes and so make a perfect Jewish nation. On the contrary, such effort tends toward pride and hypocrisy. The way to do God's will is to love others and to do to them as you would like to have them do to you. Your ideal is that of a great empire which involves the bloody triumph of the Jewish people and the terrible punishment of all their enemies. God's will will not be done on earth, until men love their enemies and are determined rather to be just than to oppress, to be brothers rather than masters.

[11] Matt. 5:44-48.

In making his own experience the test of human hopes much of his teaching became disillusionment, a correction of the expectations of his followers, an establishment of a new perspective of hope of divine salvation, a heralding of the true preparation for membership in the kingdom God would establish. It is not safe to conjecture that if he had been dealing with people of a different mood and epoch he might have expressed his ideals in other language. He never would have emerged from other social forces. One cannot, for instance, imagine John, the Evangelist, as a second Plato rather than a young Galilean, a Son of Thunder, filled with revolutionary expectations. Jesus was not dealing with abstract truth, but with young Jews on fire with revolutionary expectations which they had unified with their reli-- gious hopes.

III

Jesus not only adopted the messianic-revolutionary point of view, but he also adopted what might be called the revolutionary technique, and, like John, formed his group (*ecclesia*) of sympathizers. He chose those already full of the revolutionary spirit, who awaited the coming kingdom.* He dealt with passions and social trends rather than with the intellect. He was no lecturer to classes. He was the initiator of a group movement of such of the discontented as had his faith in God and his love for men.

How significant this new association was in the minds of its members appears in the promptness with which the vacancy, caused by the suicide of Judas, was filled.[12] From the very earliest days there was

[12] Acts 1:15-26.

no break in the new community.[13]   Jesus was in truth
an agitator.   His organization of the Twelve and of
the Seventy was for the purpose of systematized
propaganda.   But here he faced the inability of the
very persons he was drawing into a movement to
appreciate his real purposes.   He himself saw clearly
that he was playing with fire—nay, that he had come
to cast fire on the earth.   Unless he could persuade
these swarming masses and ambitious intimates that
the ideal for which he stood was not what they thought
he represented, his very movement would involve him
against his will in political uprising.   The situation in
which Jesus the agitator found himself was potential
tragedy.

His point of contact with the religious life of the
people was in the range of revolutionary hopes, but
these, when recast for his own use, were too absolutely
moral and non-resistant for those he taught.

The early appeal of Jesus was to the masses for the
purpose of selecting kindred spirits to compose this
following.   His position was parodoxical.   On the
one side he became a center of popular agitation and
crowds, but on the other side he refused to utilize the
crowds for revolutionary organization or mob violence.
Such a method must have seemed to men favoring
direct action wasteful and futile; to those responsible
for the social order it must have appeared ominous.
To them anything like popular agitation and crowd
psychology threatened society.

Nor was their apprehension without justification.
Those expectant revolutionists who gathered about
Jesus, and awaited his establishment of the new
empire which God assured, never looked upon him as

[13] Acts 2:41-47; 4:32-35.

a mere teacher of social reform. The more one considers his history, the more obvious does this fact, so unpalatable to many interpreters, appear. That which bound his disciples together was not a school of thought, but the expectation that Jesus would assume the messianic rule. It was on this faith he built his group.[14] On their part, they attached to him their own transcendental nationalism. They believed that he was the Christ incognito. Each day they felt might be the dawn of the Great Day when he would restore the kingdom to Israel. They even quarreled about the offices they might hold in the new empire.

Thus we do not see in Jesus the instigator primarily of social change or one who discussed morals in general. He was correcting a dynamic idealism already existent. His teaching is intended not for the reflective, but the active soul. Those to whom he still appeals are men and women who want God's will done in the ending of injustice, and who count their lives cheap if goodwill can be put in control of human affairs. To a group of such persons in his own day he spoke with warning and with inspiration, but not as a maker of social programs. He transformed the revolutionary spirit into a new moral attitude pregnant with social implications. For indifferent souls he had and has no message except to abandon indifference and share in his hope for a better social order prepared for those ready to impregnate conduct with the goodwill of God.

[14] Matt. 16:18. The translation "church" is misleading.

III.

JESUS ON SOCIAL ATTITUDES

Jesus reshaped a revolutionary mass psychology by the instruction given a group devoted to him. Any discovery of its content must inevitably follow the line of sound historical criticism, for none of our gospels is uninterpreted narrative. The materials which the gospels came by a process of selection to contain give plenty of evidence that in the course of its transmission across two or three generations, Christian tradition was unconsciously as well as deliberately interpreted by Christian teachers' and transcribers.

After all caution has been observed, it is not difficult to find what is beyond fair question Jesus' thought, though we may not be so sure of his precise words.* If we once place Jesus in the social and economic milieu of his times, only incidental differences are to be discovered between what is more probably his thought and what is more probably the interpretation of his disciples. That the little group about him never completely grasped his point of view is repeatedly evidenced in the gospel narrative, but that Jesus thought like a modern liberal theologian or sociologist is impossible.

But it is easy to overdo this historical criticism and unconsciously to presuppose mechanical standards of judgment. Though the beliefs of the early church as to what Jesus taught cannot be ruthlessly detached from his thought because a modern critic would have thought otherwise, it is unsafe historical practice to say that a great soul cannot pass beyond the beliefs of the period from which he emerged, however indebted to them he may have been. And certainly Jesus cannot be reduced by any Procrustean use of historical conditions to one who never rose above the level of contemporary thought. Otherwise he would have been only another unknown.

Sharing the messianic revolutionary psychology of his people, and gathering a group of those already possessed of a desire for a new world order, Jesus, like every leader, was forced to determine the particular social attitude which he should evoke in his followers. In this determination he was laying a foundation for social institutions, for they are the all but inevitable precipitate of attitudes.* He was not discussing virtue in the abstract, but human passions and hopes. He was joined by those who believed not only that God was about to establish a new world order, but that they themselves were the blessed minority who would especially benefit by the establishment of that order. Such a group, like all possessors of the revolutionary complex, on the one side was acquisitive in that it sought rights and advantages and, on the other hand, was liable to be brutal. Men who have suffered injustice have always been ready to exact terrible payment from their oppressors. Revolutions are not made of rosewater.

Jesus believed the opposite.

I

If we are really to understand Jesus we must not regard him as primarily interested in setting forth a system. His real aim was practical—the preparation of men for the kingdom, the coming of which they already expected. He was not concerned with truth for truth's sake. He was not a philosopher but an organizer of a group on fire with radical hopes. His final teaching was for them.

The failure to recognize this simple fact accounts for much needless discussion of the teaching of Jesus. In order to find general social directions men have undertaken, by a severe criticism of the documents, not only to distinguish between the teaching which comes from him and that which represents the early Christians' belief as to what he had taught, but also to speak as if he were engaged in general religious instruction something after the fashion of Socrates and Plato.[1]

In reality there are two strata in the teaching of Jesus: that intended for those not his adherents and that given to the group of sympathizers he had attracted from the masses.[*]

His teaching of those not his followers was a call

[1] This would be an overstatement if the results of Sharman, *The Teaching of Jesus about the Future,* were to be adopted. According to Sharman, Jesus foresaw the destruction of Jerusalem and the rise of messianic claimants as elements threatening the national well-being. As over against this, he believed that the kingdom of God would be "the ultimate product of certain forces which require favorable conditions and long time for their complete outworking." The conditions within his own generation were so favorable for the working of these forces that some of his disciples "would live to see development of the kingdom not now expected by them." The Day of Judgment, Sharman believes, is not in the teaching of Jesus proper, but is traceable to other sources. Practically all the strictly eschatological teachings of Jesus are centered around the coming of the Son of Man which by his disciples came to be identified on the one hand with the destruction of Jerusalem and on the other with the kingdom of God. The most significant element here is the distinction which Sharman makes between the destruction of Jerusalem and the coming of the Son of Man and the kingdom of God.

to realize the approach of God's active control of
human affairs. Like John, he began his ministry with
the call, "The kingdom of God is at hand; repent and
believe the good news." [2] There is no indication that
this call to repentance was accompanied by any
detailed moral teaching. At the beginning of his
work in Galilee his address in the synagogue at
Nazareth was also to the effect that the time was fulfilled for the beginning of the messianic era.[3] The
result of this preaching was to separate his hearers
into those who were ready to believe in his message
and those who were not. Of the former he organized
a group of intimates who were those to be specially
instructed and sent forth as heralds of the same message. And this division between those of different attitudes he expected to the end of his career.[4]

As the crowd gathered about him, he not only called
them to repentance, but spoke to them of the real
nature of the kingdom which they might expect. Sometimes this was in parables, a form of literature which
he adopted with the distinct purpose of protecting his
message from those that might misuse it.[5] He thus
made a sharp distinction between the people in general
and his group of friends who had the right to know the
"mysteries of the kingdom." Doubtless one reason for
the adoption of the use of analogies was the desire to
protect himself against any action that might savor
of political revolt.[6] But it is also clear that he expected
that there would be among the crowds that heard him

[2] Mk. 1:14, 15.
[3] Lk. 4:14-23.
[4] Matt. 10:34-39; 24:32-41; 25:1-13.
[5] Mk. 4:10-12; Matt. 13:10-17.
[6] A memory of this fear is to be found in Jn. 6:15. That the
anxiety was not without basis is to be seen in the charge by which
he was brought forth to trial before Pilate.

those who would perceive his real purpose and become his followers, ready for instruction.[7] The general character of these public announcements is thus a call to interest in his mission. If a man did not believe that the kingdom of God was close at hand, he would not be ready to welcome Jesus' further teaching. If a man was not willing to abandon his family and friends, he was not ready to be one of the immediate group about Jesus. Thus Jesus first attracted and then sifted those who were eager for the coming of the kingdom of God.

There was another appeal which Jesus made to the crowds that gathered about him, his power to cure the sick. Lacking, as his contemporaries did, any scientific knowledge of disease, they naturally accounted for its appearance by reference to devils, the visible representatives, men thought, of the kingdom of Satan. How far this belief in demonology extended is apparent to all those acquainted with the history of the period. Mental diseases in particular were regarded as indication of demoniacal possession. Thus any ability to heal disease, especially "demoniacs," would naturally be regarded not only as an evidence of supernatural power, but an indication of being either the prince of the evil forces or the representative of the kingdom of God. The cures wrought by Jesus became thus an appeal to the people in general as an indication of more than prophetic power on his own part. He declared that this power of casting out demons showed that the kingdom of God had drawn nigh. His power over Satan was thus evidence not only of his messianic office, but of his performing mes-

[7] This is the natural implication of Mk. 4:23, "Any man that hath ears to hear, let him hear." Cf. Matt. 13:9; Mk. 4:9; Lk. 8:8; Matt. 11:15; Lk. 14:35.

sianic work. The literary and religious authorities, however, regarded him as a representative of Beelzebub, the prince of the demons.[8] Such an interpretation gave occasion for Jesus to make public announcement that he represented the kingdom of God, but he followed such teaching only by general admonitions.[9] He left the crowds to put their own interpretation on what he himself regarded as the exercise of a messianic power which waited God's time for full expression.

The chief appeal which he made to the people at large, however, was not so much the miracle as the call to repentance. That was indeed the sign of Jonah.[10] And repentance was the obverse of a trust in God's love. Poor and simple though a man might be, he could enjoy the divine fatherliness if he chose. God cared for a lost soul as a shepherd cared for a lost sheep, a housewife for a lost coin, a father for a lost son; and there was joy in heaven, Jesus declared, when the lost was found.[11]

The replies of Jesus to inquiries from other than his immediate following were determined by the attitude of the questioner. If the question came from hostility its answer was likely to be polemic, or one of warning. His first interest was to discover whether the inquirer showed potential loyalty to the expected kingdom. When this loyalty was present, as in Zacchaeus, the person became at once a follower, ready for the more specific teaching as to conduct consistent with such faith. Jesus refused to be, so to speak, a general practitioner in morals.*

[8] Mk. 3:22-30.
[9] Such a view does not attempt to answer the critical question as to whether Matt. 12:33-37 and 43-45 are associated with the immediately preceding discussion of the unpardonable sin.
[10] Matt. 12:38-42, 16:4; Lk. 11:29-32.
[11] Lk. 15:1-31.

II

This deliberate choice of method brings into sharp relief the necessity of understanding the attitudes presupposed by such teachings as he gave his followers rather than the masses.

1. Below all his teaching was the sympathy which identified Jesus with the unfortunate, the poor, and the oppressed. He saw them as they saw themselves, sheep without a shepherd, sick that must be cured, despised who must be given self-respect, discontented who must hope, futureless who must have faith in a better day to come. Jesus is out of perspective when placed against any other background than this attitude. He had no smug confidence in a prosperity-giving providence. He has suffered the fate of the prophets. The respectability of his own day killed him and the respectability of our day has appropriated him. But he has no message of comfort for those who substitute self-complacency for moral discontent. He was not sent to call the righteous, but the sinners, to repentance. The crowds heard him gladly because they saw in him one of themselves who brought them a message that set no conditions of learning or social status.

This sympathy with the unprivileged, this participation in their hopes, explains Jesus' call to sacrifice. His central message is to those with privileges, and it is that of voluntary participation and sharing. There is in his words no call to thrift or demand for rights. He was not a labor leader or a leader of revolt. Living in the midst of revolutionists, leading those who shared his revolutionary hopes because of their faith in God, he did not cheapen his appeal by promising wealth

or comfort. The true riches which he promised were
the enjoyment of the love of God and the exercise of
a love like his. A dilettante in morals could possess
the Age-life he sought only when in desperate earnestness he gave his property away.[12]

2. The basic attitude which Jesus sought to develop in
those who joined his group was that of absolute faith
in the goodwill of God. This was central in his own
experience. When once he had discovered what was
the will of the Father he could find joy, and promise
to those who would follow his teaching and bear his
yoke the same peace of soul.[13] This faith in the goodwill of God was not derived from any hope of the
speedy coming of the Kingdom. The latter belief
might have been accompanied with the fear of God's
severity. This love of God Jesus could see in nature [14]
and in human relations.[15] It could be trusted to provide for even the humblest needs of those who were
preparing for the kingdom of God. For them there
was no need of anxious thought.[16] In the synoptic
gospels this faith has no touch of mysticism. It is a
trust born of a conviction. Possessing it, one prays
and expects to receive good gifts. Jesus, however,
does not tell his disciples to pray for moral strength
or spiritual qualities. He is ethical rather than con-
templative. He does not promise men new emotions,
although when one is grateful to God for forgiveness
it is evident that divine forgiveness has been acquired.[17]
His primary test is whether a person has the same sort
of attitude in human relations that God has in his.
His followers are to be "perfect as their Heavenly

[12] Mk. 10:17-22 and parallels.
[13] Matt. 11:25-30.
[14] Matt. 6:26-30.
[15] Lk. 11:5-13.
[16] Matt. 6:31-34.
[17] Lk. 7:36-50.

Father is perfect," [18] that is, possessed of sacrificial social-mindedness.* Without this faith in God the ethics of Jesus would never have been taught.

3. In the character of God lies the justification of goodwill and love on the part of those who await the kingdom. Such an attitude is the very contradiction to acquisitiveness, force, hyprocrisy, lust, and all the other attitudes that lead a person to treat others as means rather than ends. Such love is not to be identified with emotion, although emotion must, of course, be involved within it. It is a willingness to treat others as persons rather than as means, and to make one's own good coördinate with the good of all others involved in the same situation. Men are to do to others as they would like others to do to them; they are to love people whom they do not like. They can develop a moral attitude which is superior to any passing sentiment. In the course of time it may be that the proper sentiment may follow the moral good, but Jesus did not teach his immediate followers to wait for such an emotion. They were to take the initiative in establishing friendly relations with enemies and "brothers" alike.[19] Forgiveness was to be as frequent as repentance.[20] Duty was no measure of social service.[21]

Such teaching was given by him only to those already committed to his announcement of the approaching kingdom of God. With them, anything that assured their entrance into the kingdom would arouse emotional interest. If Jesus had bidden them turn to arms, their enthusiasm would have made them

[18] Lk. 6:36; Matt. 5:48.   [20] Matt. 18:21-35.
[19] Matt. 5:23-26, 44; 18:15-17.   [21] Matt. 17:5-10.

militant, but he told them to treat their enemies and their oppressors in the way of love. Proper hope and trust would give them the necessary motive to attempt to put his teachings into operation.

Jesus recognized that such an attitude involved the probability of suffering. Devotion to it would arouse the enmity of those who held other views. He foretold frankly the outcome in his own case and theirs.[22] Whether they ever fully grasped his meaning prior to his execution may well be doubted, but after his death his followers committed themselves to this teaching. They turned from acquisitiveness and violence, preferring to be poor and to die rather than violate the spirit of Jesus which they possessed.

III

It is his elevation of love that gives Jesus his place as a social teacher. Yet it has never been made central in the theology of the Christian church. There is not a creed or a confession that emphasizes it. The belief in God the Father became a belief in the first and unbegotten Person of a metaphysical Trinity. Belief in his love has been replaced by an appeal to God's mercy in the name of Christ who died for sinners. The belief in the triumph of a kingdom of love and righteousness has been replaced by expectation of joy in heaven or torture in hell. That is to say, in the course of its development the group of followers whom Jesus inducted into the mysteries of the kingdom has given less attention to the teaching of Jesus than to the nature of his person and his work as an atoning Savior. To be sure, attempts of men like St. Benedict and St. Francis to make the teaching of Jesus dominant in a

[22] Mk. 13:9, 11-13. Cf. Matt. 24:9, 13; Jn. 15:21; 16:2.

community of spiritually loyal persons have resulted
in institutional interests and spiritual exclusiveness,
yet Christians in their vital religion have always recognized his revelation of God as love and heard his call
to make love an element of their lives. For the religion
of Christians has never been restricted to their dogmas.

But if it be hard for those who are committed to
faith in Jesus to appreciate and apply his central teaching as to love, how much more difficult it is for those
who have no such loyalty, who repudiate his leadership
and see only the imperfect morality of those who profess Christian ideals! To Nietzsche, love is a sign of
weakness and the will to power is more to be desired.
To men who have shaped the destinies of nations,
power and deceit have seemed far more practicable
than arbitration or the sacrificial giving of justice.
There can be no compromise at this point. A man is
for Jesus or against him. If love is not in the nature
of things it is weakness; but if it is what Jesus taught,
it is the ultimate dynamic.

Thus unexpectedly the indifference of Jesus to moral
opportunism, due to his belief in the speedy coming
of the kingdom, is seen to be anything but an obses-
sion of grandeur. When he deals with concrete situations in life, like marriage, forgiveness, alms, conversation, epithets, it is always with the absolute ideal
involved in such action that he is concerned. An attitude as distinguished from an ideal belongs in the
realm of motive and mind-sets rather than in the world
of specific duties. One discovers his attitude by facing
some task or ideal or goal.[23] Like produces like. Men
do not gather grapes from thorns or figs from thistles.

[23] Charters, *The Teaching of Ideals*, 34, 35. See also Dewey,
Moral Principles in Education; Tufts, *The Real Business of Living;*
Smith, *Principles of Christian Living.*

From a specific act one may thus learn the mind-set or character·or attitude of the actor and, conversely, individual acts are the expression of some attitude or attitudes. To unify action in accordance with an ideal that is social, and to develop the attitude of response to the ideal which shall remain constant and unifying in the midst of the variety of life, is the center of Jesus' method of teaching. His ideal is the character of God as Father; his dominant attitude is goodwill or love.*

The evidence that the "will to love" is superior to the "will to power" lies in the very nature of our world. Jesus rather than his critics was near to cosmic reality. The expression of the supreme law of nature has been called "creative coördination."[24] That is to say nature, while producing individuals, also produces combinations, and gives to individuals real efficiency only in combination with others. Love is the expression of this coördination in the realm of personality. By it the highest values have arisen in human life and without it human society would disintegrate. When Jesus thus emphasizes love he is no more appealing to human weakness and sentimentality than if he had told men that if they were to walk uprightly they must coördinate their actions with the force of gravity. His exposition of the relations of men with nature was naturally unscientific, but his reading of human life and his own consciousness led him to the perception that the coördination of the individual's good with the welfare of the total group in which he acts is the expression of the divine will, that is to say, of the activity with which all life must conform. Love is a

[24] Pupin, *The New Reformation;* Mathews, *Contributions of Science to Religion.*

cosmic law. Selfishness is a violation of the law of coördination through subjection of the group welfare to the individual just as truly as the subjection of the good of individuals to that of the group means moral weakness.*

Love as Jesus sets it forth may therefore be described as an urge to social coöperation in which the coöperating parties treat each other as persons. The welfare of the individual is furthered by the coöperation of all those who are members of the group. They can act egoistically only at the cost of suffering in the group. The satisfactions which individuals might gain are furthered at the expense of the welfare of others. But when men undertake to express the attitude of coördination in group action social institutions emerge, for institutions are one of the means which preserve and socialize attitudes. By them values are passed on from generation to generation. They are indispensable in proportion as they enable group action to favor the personal worth of individuals. When once that function ceases and the institution becomes an end rather than a means, it must be transformed or replaced by some other institution better fitted for the development of personal needs. The attitudes which an institution organizes and preserves precede the institution itself. The desire to fight is prior to the organization of armies; the desire for wealth is prior to the organization of commerce; the desire for order is prior to government; and the desire for offspring is prior to the family. The value of these institutions must be determined, therefore, by discovering how far the attitude they preserve is calculated to build up personal values by social coördination, how far the institution is able itself to further these values in the midst of an ever

more complicated social order, and how far both attitudes and institutions are in accord with the will of
the cosmic God. By this test the teaching of Jesus is
to be judged. Good trees bring forth good fruit. Love
must beget institutions of social value.

IV

It follows that the two attitudes to which Jesus was
particularly opposed were acquisitiveness and vindic-
tiveness. The first, as always in the revolutionary psychology, was to be found in the spirit of his fellow
countrymen. They wanted to acquire power and rights
and happiness. They wanted to make their oppressors
suffer and called upon God to avenge wrongs done His
people. The two attitudes are alike in that the satisfaction of the individual is made superior to the good
of the total group to which he belongs. Each prompts
one to seek gain at the expense of others. Institutions
that preserve and express such attitudes are to be
destroyed or transformed by those who would treat
Jesus seriously.

Yet these two attitudes are among the most potent
in human life. The desire for wealth lies back of most
human undertakings, while the determination to gain
rights is almost a synonym of revolution. Similarly
in the case of hatreds. To get people to hate together
is to get them to fight together against the object of
their dislike. Every successful leader of men has known
how to unify his followers by arousing antagonism to
others. These antagonisms have generally been clothed
in some form of idealism, but are really dependent
upon the strength of a common hatred of persons, institutions, or social conditions.

Every demagogue knows how to arouse these attitudes, and they were probably never more pronounced than in the time of Jesus. Men were presently to appeal to them in a search for independence and national revenge. Jesus obviously knew their power, and sought to sublimate them, though he well knew that he might become their victim.

But there was a third attitude less obviously danger-ous which Jesus repudiated vigorously, namely, the restriction of God's favor to those who know and observe ecclesiastical statutes. In his criticism of this third attitude Jesus showed himself anything but a quietist. Like all those who voice the revolutionary attitude, he was a controversialist. While he dis-tinguished indignation from hatred and did not resort to arms, he did resort to bitter words. His criticism of the Pharisees amounts to excoriation. They are whited sepulchers, hypocrites, devourers of widows' houses, neither entering into the kingdom of God nor permit-ting others to enter in, making proselytes into children of hell. Because of his assaults, the term "Pharisee" has lost its better meanings and become a synonym of insincerity and ecclesiastical arrogance.

The basis of this opposition to Pharisaism is diffi-cult to find by comparing his detached teachings with those of Pharisee rabbis. In point of literary perfec-tion his sayings are superior, but they are not without parallels from Jewish teachers.[25] Furthermore, the

[25] This point is emphasized strongly by Jewish writers who justly feel that they have a right to claim Jesus as theirs. Their method of appropriation is to insist that there is no difference between the genuine teachings of Jesus and Pharisaism, that all his great sayings were expositions of current teachings of Pharisees, and that therefore he could not have been opposed by them, much less brought to his death by them. See especially Klausner, *Jesus of Nazareth;* also Herford, *The Pharisees,* p. 115sq. Much of this comparison, how-ever, makes it impossible to understand the facts of the Christian movement.

Pharisees were themselves a lay movement in religion which had broken with the conservative spirit of the priestly Sadducees, had made the law include not only the whole Old Testament, and with considerable freedom had undertaken so to interpret the Old Testament as to free it from literalism. In fact, there was within the Pharisaic movement something approaching a universal note in that several rabbis refused to believe that the law could teach anything really contrary to elemental justice or the most noble spirit of the utterances of the prophets.

No understanding of the attitude of Jesus is to be gained by emphasizing the points of similarity between his teachings and those of the Pharisees. That they were at one time on friendly terms is apparent,[26] but the more one presses such similarities, the more unintelligible does the gospel narrative become. If Jesus were so thoroughly rabbinical as some writers hold, we have an entirely different Jesus with an entirely different career from anything the gospels describe.

The difficulty here is due to the effort to understand Jesus as simply a teacher among teachers. Once set in his actual historical situation, the issues between him and the Pharisees become perfectly plain. Jesus allied himself with the *am-ha-aretz,* the poor, the hungry, the sinful masses, and would naturally be sensitive to the attitudes of antagonism which had grown up between the masses and their natural leaders, the Pharisees. He was organizing a movement of those possessed of the revolutionary spirit, and the Pharisees were naturally suspicious of such activity.

But more fundamental than this was the opposition

[26] Lk. 7:36.

between Jesus' conception of a man's approach to God as determined by a man's moral attitude rather than through a highly interpreted Mosaic law (*halachah*).[27] However liberal the Pharisee may have been in his interpretation of scripture, however he may have endeavored to carry the message of his religion to the non-Jewish world, to him the law properly interpreted and observed was always the means of approach to God's favor. This position Jesus assailed.[28] Not only did he object to the details of professional interpreters which were at last to find their way into the Talmud, but he objected to the statutory law itself as incomplete.[29] It was not to pass away, but it was to be completed in an attitude of soul independent of technical biblical knowledge, to be possessed by the poorest as well as the most learned. Both alike needed to become like little children if they were to enjoy the blessings of the approaching kingdom of God.

Just when the controversy began between Jesus and the Pharisees it is difficult to say, but it was inevitable as soon as the position of Jesus was perceived. His popularity as a nonprofessional teacher among the masses, his self-assertion as a religious authority, his opposition to any limitation upon the free access of the repentant sinner to God, his minimizing of the ceremonial requirements of the religious authorities, his criticism of the laws governing the sabbath, his rejec-

[27] See Herford, *The Pharisees*, 107*sq.*; Lazarus, *The Ethics of Judaism;* Lauterback, "Ethics of the Halakah" in *Year Book of the Central Conference of American Rabbis, 1913; Sadducees and Pharisees.* See further, Jackson and Lake, *The Beginnings of Christianity*, I, 110-114.

[28] Mk. 7:1-13.

[29] Matt. 5:21-48; Mk. 7:14-23.

tion of fasting and hand-washing, would have led inevitably to mutual opposition.[30]

But whatever the origin of his break with the Pharisees, Jesus unqualifiedly condemned any limitation set to the humblest soul's enjoyment of the forgiving love of God and any justification of an act that did not spring from the attitude of goodwill. God's goodwill was the basis of confidence in the power of goodwill in men. To think of Jesus as a peaceful dreamer of idyllic utopias or a quietist meditating about abstract truth is utterly to pervert the picture which the gospels leave. Jesus did nothing to placate his critics and his opponents. On the contrary, he vehemently assailed them. They were misrepresenting God. Foreseeing that he would suffer the fate of the prophets and popular leaders, he did not undertake to soften the contrast between his organization of messianic idealism and the desire of the responsible citizens for social order based on conformity to a national and academic religion. It is this aggressiveness on the part of Jesus that gives coloring and vigor to his teaching. As a leader of a movement of those possessed of a common moral attitude, he confronted its opponents with criticism and denunciation. And he paid for his spiritual democracy* with his life.

V

Jesus' interests were centered on the production of the socially minded individual dominated by goodwill. He was not seeking to establish the kingdom of God but to prepare men to enter it. The difference between

[30] That there were thoroughly unworthy Pharisees among the associates the rabbis themselves admitted, and some of the bitterness of Jesus' criticism may have been the outgrowth of knowledge of such unworthy persons. In fact, he seems to make a distinction between the teachings of the scribes and their practices (Matt. 23:2, 3).

these opposing interpretations of his words must be at once apparent. If the chief purpose of Jesus was to establish gradually the kingdom of God, then his chief goal was a society. Such an attempt, of course, would have been thoroughly in accord with the revolutionary spirit of his time, with its strong nationalist hope. So, too, it would accord with modern attempts to set up a perfect society to which the welfare of the individual must be subjected; with the spirit of militarism which would set up social unity by the complete subjection of the individual to the control of a superior; with the spirit of those who would establish a successful industrial or commercial operation without regard to the welfare of the individual men and women involved.

There is something attractive in the idea that Jesus was committed to the establishment of a great social unity. It seems a short cut to happiness. The attempt to bring about a new society has always had its romantic appeal for the discontented. Not a few men, in despair of the normal capacities of the individual, have sought to further human welfare by collective action and by the change of social environment. Nor is it impossible to plead certain of the sayings of Jesus in behalf of this view.[31] Thus, it is said to be like

[31] I did this myself in *The Social Teaching of Jesus*, ch. iii, and the same view has been popular among socially minded clergymen. As I trust will appear as the discussion proceeds, my criticism of this view is primarily exegetical. That a better social order will arise by the following of the teaching of Jesus is of course the point of my contention, but it is one thing to say that Jesus meant this when the term "kingdom of God" is used and another to say (more accurately) that social institutions will be improved as the human material that goes into them enables them to be improved. It is one thing to say that Jesus was primarily concerned with society in general and another to say that he was interested in the social attitudes of individuals upon which a social reorganization must depend. See my *Messianic Hope in the New Testament*, ch. iii. For the other view see Rauschenbusch, *Christianity and the Social Crisis*. Peabody, *Jesus Christ and the Social Question*, emphasizes attitudes rather than exegesis.

leaven,[32] it is said to progress like grain, first the blade, then the ear, then the full kernels in the ear;[33] it is said to be "within you or among you."[34] But a fair interpretation of these terms finds in them a reference not to progress but to eschatological outcome. To make Jesus a social reformer, much more a social legislator, is to misinterpret him. He dealt with attitudes of individuals rather than with programs of society.

VI

We therefore distinguish between the central message of Jesus and his occasional application of his teachings to society as he faced it. We may, perhaps, find in his teachings interim *mores* but not an interim ideal.* That ideal was unaffected and uncaused by his belief in the immediacy of the kingdom. He was not engaged in furthering social change, much less political revolution. He was describing an absolute moral attitude as found in the will of God. He was not concerned with telling people how to proceed toward an ideal; he set forth in unqualified fashion the quality of life which the ideal demanded. The time of its fulfilment is unimportant. Facing eternity, he taught men to embody the basic character of God. The goodwill of God is not to be identified with social evolution, but is an absolute good. Just as the geometrician can discuss the nature and laws of curves which it is impossible to draw, so the kingdom of God is set forth by Jesus as that which is inherent in the divine economy. But as the circles and hyperbolas of geometry are only approximate illustrations of the absolute figures, so human conduct is only an imperfect embodiment of

[32] Matt. 13:33; Lk. 13:20, 21.   [33] Mk. 4:26-29.   [34] Lk. 17:20.

the absolute ideal. Its value is determined by the approach which it makes to that ideal.

The specific social teachings of Jesus, in so far as they exist, are to be regarded as the expression of what would be true in case the attitude of love were realized. They are not forecasts of a social process. As it proved, it became the duty of every Christian to adopt a technique which expresses the attitude of love in social institutions. An individual grows personal as he grows social, but whoever commits himself to the supreme motive of love and intelligently adopts a coöperative technique is in spirit a revolutionist like his Lord. For he looks to a new world-order that shall be the expression of that sacrificial social-mindedness and reliance upon God which constitute the attitude of Jesus himself. It was with such eager and serious souls Jesus had to do in his day, and it is only such souls who follow him to-day. For them the words of Jesus are more than a call to duty. They are the good news that love is practicable because God is love. Jesus had no illusions about men. He knew their evil side and lived in full expectation of the momentary triumph of forces of evil. But he was no disconsolate friend of man, seated like a literary Job on a garbage heap of cynical epigrams. God's goodwill was a rock on which he and all who undertook to be like him could build their house of hope and service to others. He was not calling men to a forlorn hope, but to ultimate victory. It was the Father's good pleasure to give the kingdom to those who possessed the spirit of brothers. The little group who gathered about Jesus was pitifully small, but it was to grow like the mustard seed. It might be poor and hungry and sad, but none the less it was to be congratulated, for it was under the guidance of a Heavenly Father, and possessed of forces before which the gates of hell would fall. It is such a group that has always sought to preserve the attitude of Jesus in social life, embodying it, sometimes ignorantly and always imperfectly, in social institutions.

IV

JESUS AS THE EXPONENT OF SOCIAL ATTITUDES

A FOUNDER of a movement does more than teach his followers. Whether he wills it or not, he becomes an example. If he flouts the responsibility his hypocrisy injures his cause; if he embodies his ideals he becomes an inspiration. Jesus was no exception to this rule. His life became an example because men saw he followed his own teaching. If he told a would-be disciple to leave his home, he himself had no place in which to lay his head; if he told his disciples to trust the Heavenly Father for their daily needs, he himself was supported by friends; if he said that some would be unmarried for the sake of a kingdom of heaven, he himself was celibate; if he told his disciples to avoid conflict with civil authorities, he himself refused to be involved in rebellion; if he told men to choose life rather than mere living, he himself died on the cross rather than distrust his mission. His teachings were thus the vocalizing of his experience.* The Christ who "for our sakes became poor" is the chief heritage of the Christian community. He was the Son of Man—the type of the kingdom he announced, who came to minister and to give his life as a ransom for many.[1]

How, then, did Jesus embody the attitude of love he saw in God and urged upon his followers?

[1] Matt. 20:28.

65

I

It may seem gratuitous to deny that Jesus in his embodiment of the attitude of love was an ascetic or semi-ascetic. So far has the pendulum swung away from the medieval conception of holiness that it often seems as if the chief need of to-day were a Savonarola who should fascinate us into new burnings of novels and gewgaws. But none the less, so ineradicable is the suspicion that religion is in some way a sort of counter-agent for the joys of life that it is often forgotten that the founder of Christianity came eating and drinking, in the envious eyes of contemporary religious teachers a winebibber and a glutton.[2] Goodwill like that of the Father did not make Jesus an eccentric. In fact he was so normal that his career was darkened by men's distrust. John the Baptist was quite another man. The prophet's dress and the pauper's food, together with his sternly ascetic preaching, gave him popularity.[3] Even nowadays it is by no means so easy to attract the crowds by respectability as by sensation. It is easier to preach against fashionable extravagances and social absurdities than to exhibit gentlemanly unobtrusiveness in goodness. Too many men yet measure their goodness by their sense of deprivation, making misery the thermometer of holiness.

[2] Matt. 11:19.

[3] The hold that John had upon the minds of his contemporaries is to be seen not only in the oldest sources of our gospels (see for instance Mark 1:1-8) but also in the pages of Josephus (*Ant.* 18; 5:2). By the latter writer the misfortunes that filled the later days of Herod Antipas are said to have been popularly regarded as judgments for the killing of John. Even if, as very likely is the case, this reference to John has been subjected to interpolations, it stands on much securer critical ground that Josephus' reference to Jesus himself (*Ant.* 18; 3:3). Other tributes to the permanence of John's influence are seen in Acts 18:25; 19:3.

In the Fourth Gospel Jesus begins his Galilean ministry by providing a wedding company with wine.[4] And this was only one instance out of many in which Jesus used social gatherings for the furthering of his mission. In fact much of his teaching was connected with dining, the social meal giving either the occasion or the analogy for his thought. He distinctly rejected fasting as a religious form,[5] and destroyed all ceremonial distinctions in food.[6] If sometimes he fasted,[7] it was from no desire to acquire merit; and if he withdrew into solitude it was for a season of prayer from which he returned the more devotedly to public life.[8]

But while the pleasures of social life are good in themselves, they are not to be ends in themselves. The life of love depends on something more than food.[9] That something which can make eating and drinking goods subordinate to some greater goods is the spirit of brotherliness which uses them to further the happiness of others. The member of the new movement was not to flee the world,[10] but was rather to stay in it as a source of light and life.[11] Social life was shown by the life of Jesus to be the normal life of men.

II

It is not to magnify trivialities if attention be called to the attitude of Jesus toward the conventionalities

---

[4] Jn. 2:1-12. It is impossible to think that the conditions of this story are fulfilled by the assumption that the wine provided by Jesus was non-alcoholic.

[5] Matt. 9:14; 6:17, 18. In this connection his picture of the boasting Pharisee (Lk. 18:10) is especially striking.

[6] Mk. 7:17, 19.

[7] Matt. 4:12; Lk. 4:2.

[8] Mk. 6:46sq.; Matt. 14:23sq.; Lk. 9:28.

[9] Matt. 6:25.

[10] Jn. 17:15.

[11] Matt. 5:14.

of life. His social-mindedness was always in evidence.
It is of course possible that a man should be thoroughly
good and worthy of respect and yet be totally indifferent to the requirements of good society. But no cultured man wants a boor as his religious teacher any
more than he would accept a filthy saint as his savior.
Jesus was careful about those matters which in his day
indicated the gentleman. Though a poor man and
counting clothes as at best but a secondary good [12] he
seems to have been well dressed [13] and to have followed the ordinary dictates of the Jewish fashions
except, perhaps, in the matter of phylacteries. [14] His
sensitiveness to matters of common civility appears in
the words forced from him by the rudeness of a host
who allowed conceit to drive out politeness. [15] That
Judas should have betrayed him by a kiss added bitterness to the cup he was forced to drink. [16] These matters
are, of course, of small importance as they stand by
themselves, but they gain in significance when they
are seen to represent an attitude of mind.

To Jesus love was not sentimentality, nor did it
destroy self-respect. Whether from sensitiveness or
some other motive, Jesus, with all his love and eagerness to attract men, never cheapened himself by indiscriminate friendships. His brief career was marked by

[12] Matt. 6:25, 28.
[13] Jn. 19:23.
[14] Matt. 9:20.   The rabbis seem to have been as supreme in
fashion as in religion. We know from their decisions not only the
names and styles of the garments worn by Jesus but also the order
in which they should be put on and their relative importance. (The
authority on the subject of Jewish costume is Brüll, *Trachten der
Juden.* See also Edersheim, *Life and Times of Jesus the Messiah,*
621*sq.*)   The fact to be especially noticed in this connection is the
probability that Jesus wore the *tsitsith* or tassels on his *tallith* or
outer garment.
[15] Lk. 7:36-50.
[16] Lk. 22:48.

great reserve; indeed, it seems a series of withdrawals from promiscuous popularity in order that he might establish a few intense friendships. To the outer crowd he carefully refused to show the depths of his character; to the wide circle of mercurial "believers" he revealed hardly more of himself; to the Twelve as a whole he showed as much of himself as he could educate them to appreciate. And only one of the Twelve was "the disciple Jesus loved." Some men are at their best in public; others among their intimates. The first come dangerously near acting; the latter are seldom insincere. Jesus belonged to the second class. While he knew something of the intoxicating joy that comes to the orator, his choicest teachings are those given in some conversation. Thus it came about that while he was followed by multitudes he was loved by only a few. But these few preserved his spirit and example for the ages.

III

Because he thus chose his friends it would be absurd to say that Jesus recognized the existence of social classes. He was democratic in spirit, however conscious of his supreme vocation. His limitations of intimacy were not based upon accidental differences. Nor do his teachings imply such classes. So long as men were bad, so long they could not be other than selfish. All of their efforts could be only for private advantage. Wealth could not fail to be other than a means for ungenerous enjoyment.[17] Prayer would lengthen itself immoderately that the Creator might be wearied into submission to the more persistent will.[18] Social customs would be only new agencies for forcing an

[17] Lk. 12:16-21.   [18] Matt. 7:7.

indebted acquaintance to repay hospitality in kind.[19]
Jesus saw all this clearly; and he saw its inevitable
outgrowth: the stratification of men according to their
ability to fulfil these purely materialistic conditions.
With such stratification fraternity would be impossible.
Therefore he who attempted to exalt himself would be
humiliated.[20]   In the new community no man was to
be called master, for they were all brethren,[21] serving
one another.   And not only were they brothers one of
another, they were his brothers as well, the least as
well as the greatest.   No more striking lesson of social
equality was ever given man than that of the Christ
going about with a towel washing the feet of his followers.[22]   So emphatically does Jesus preach the gospel
of equality as to say that, in the coming order, the last
should be first and the first last.[23]

Yet he does not, like some modern champions of
the doctrine, attempt the sudden destruction of all traditional distinctions.   There is undoubtedly need of
such iconoclasts, but that constructive spirit which is
everywhere noticeable in the career of Jesus is present
here.   Jesus belonged to the artisan class,[24] and knew
what it was to feel the contempt of the professional
teachers of his people.[25]   He did not hesitate to confess the advantage possessed by the educated man,[26]
but he never allowed these facts to lead him into tirade
against other men's advantages.

It is, however, by no means inconsistent with this

[19] Lk. 14:12.
[20] Matt. 23:12.
[21] Matt. 23:8.
[22] Jn. 13:1-10.
[23] Matt. 19:30.   No sentence of Jesus seems to have made deeper
impression on his hearers.   It is constantly repeated in the gospels.
[24] Mk. 6:3.
[25] Matt. 13:54-56.
[26] Matt. 13:52.

attitude that he recognized that as society was constituted men must of necessity be divided into servants
and employers. He said nothing that condemned such
a relation, and indeed at times spoke of it as a most
natural thing.[27] This is the attitude of any practical
man who champions ideals. Your amateur reformer
would dissolve society into its elements. Like Robes-
pierre and other doctrinaires, he will break with the
past, even though he brings the bones of departed
kings to the lime-pit. But Jesus was never so crude
a thinker as to imagine that because a man loves
humanity he must disintegrate society as a step toward
a happier recombination. And therefore he did not
destroy all social conventionalities or a traditional division of labor.

But to be a servant is not to be any less a man or,
provided it is really the case, any less the equal of any
man in another calling. If nothing that goes into a
man can defile him, certainly no necessary work is dis-
honorable. Jesus the carpenter and the son of a carpenter became Jesus the Christ; his seemingly Fal-
staffian army of fishermen, tax collectors, and reformed
revolutionists became in a few months the pillars of
the church at Jerusalem and the evangelists of the
nation. Indeed, nothing is more admirable than the
catholicity of sympathy and practice that made him
the friend of all sorts of people. Such democracy
scandalized the aristocratic teachers and preachers and
lawyers of his own day. How often did they rail
against him as a friend of the publican and the sinner!
In their sight he could be no prophet, since he dared
receive a repentant woman of the town.[28] With them
as with all legalists the temptation was strong to judge

[27] Lk. 17:7-10; Matt. 10:24.   [28] Lk. 7:39sq.

harshly and superficially of all unusual characters, and
their criticism of the generous habits of Jesus was a
testimony to the openness of his sympathy with honest
effort at reform and his disregard of all artificial distinctions.   To the Pharisees the common people who
knew not the law were accursed; to Jesus they were
possible members of God's kingdom.[29]

And his words were the echoes of his life.   One of
the proofs of his Messiahship that the disciples of John
were to carry back to their unfortunate master was
that the gospel was being preached to the poor.[30]   As
he himself ate with the publican and the sinner, so
when a man would give a feast Jesus bade him invite
the lame and the halt and the blind.[31]   Could social
equality combined with an avoidance of self-seeking
be more strikingly enforced?

IV

Probably the strongest objection to the recognition
in actual life of this ideal of Jesus is the ineradicable
conviction that social equality is impracticable.   Men
have dreamed of it and have died, leaving their dreams
to the laughter of their times and the libraries of their
descendants.   These words of Jesus are beautiful, but
so are those of More and Rousseau—and no more
visionary.   Men are not equal and fraternity is a word
for orators and French public buildings.

So men say, or think if they keep silent.

But Jesus does not claim that men in the world
to-day are physiologically equal.   There are the lame
and the halt.   Nor are they mentally on an equality.
There are men to whom one talent could be entrusted,

[29] Jn. 7:49; Matt. 11:28.   [31] Lk. 14:12sq.
[30] Matt. 11:5; Lk. 7:22.

and those to whom five and ten.[32] Nor does Jesus so far fall into the class of nature-philosophers as to teach that because men are to be brothers they are therefore to be twins. The equality of fraternity does not consist in duplication of powers, but in the free enjoyment and the exercise of love.

Further, according to the new social standard of Jesus two men are equal, not because they have equal claims upon each other, but because they owe equal duties to each other. His gospel was not a new Declaration of Rights, but a Declaration of Duties.[33]

V

It may be objected that Jesus passed over those claims for justice and equality which to-day are urged with an ever-increasing passion. But he was not oblivious to the injustice suffered by those who had not shared sufficiently in the good things of life. He never promised men heaven as a recompense for submission to such injustice. He was the friend of the oppressed. No man's teaching has been more potent in forcing the strong to yield to the weak, the rich to the poor, the noble to the lowly. But Jesus was far less interested in the rights than in the obligations of men. It matters little that logically the two conceptions are complementary. Practically there is a vast difference between the bald demand of men or classes for things due them, and that extension of privilege which sympathy and a sense of obligation may induce a favored man or class to effect. Of the two, it is easier to arouse

[32] Matt. 25:14-30; Lk. 19:12-27.
[33] The constitutional history of the French Revolution is a commentary upon this position of Jesus. It was a new age that replaced the *Declaration des Droits de l'Homme et du Citoyen* of the constitution of 1791, with the *Declaration des Droits et ces Devoirs de l'Homme et du Citoyen* of the constitution of Fructidor, 1795.

the demand for justice, but no one who knows the
crimes that have been committed in the name of
liberty, and the hereditary hatreds that have been the
outgrowth of struggles after rights, need be told that
the victories of justice leave scars as ineradicable as its
demands are righteous. It was from some appreciation
of this that Jesus even in his friendship with the poor
made duty paramount to rights. The Jew was ready
enough to grant the rights of a neighbor—when once
neighborship had been defined and proved. In the
estimation of Jesus, to be a neighbor was not to have
rights that put others under obligation to oneself, but
to be conscious of duties. Not the wounded traveler,
but the Levite and the priest and the Samaritan needed
to show the spirit of the neighbor.[34]   Indeed, to one
who has been assailed loudly with the evils of to-day's
economic inequalities, it is at first sight surprising
to find Jesus so indifferent to much that to-day's
reformers emphasize so strenuously. But to urge the
poor man to struggle after wealth might be to spur
him to selfishness as deep as that of the rich man
against whom he struggles. Poverty as experienced by
Jesus did not involve a discontent that endangered
love. It might be necessary to subdue nature, to make
natural forces the servants of production, but wealth
and sensuousness and selfishness, Jesus saw, go hand
in hand.[35]   Mere bigness is not goodness, and enthusiasm over bank accounts is not the spirit of the
Master. Life is more than food and fraternity more
than wealth.[36]   Social agitators, John the Baptists of
economics, are needed. We may yet count Karl Marx
and Lassalle among the prophets, but what sort of
fraternity would a Christ have established whose

[34] Lk. 10:25-37.   [35] Lk. 8:14.   [36] Lk. 12:23.

evangel was a political economy and whose sympathy was set forth in a program?

He had experienced a greater good than the possession of wealth—participation in the kingdom of God. For all who were to be its members there was no inequality of opportunity, because love was for all and to be enjoyed. This he knew from experience.

It would have been a sorry message for humanity that stopped short of this recognition of the supremacy of personal values over all goods. The attitude of Jesus was determined by these ultimate values; to him all other matters were incidental.[37] For them he was ready to make the supreme sacrifice when the choice was inevitable. The same heroism he expected of those who came after him. He had no patience with moral procrastination.[38] He himself was too loyal to his absolute ideals to permit halfway measures on the part of his followers. They could submit to evil, but they were not to compromise with it. They could die as loyal children of the kingdom, but they could not trifle with words or deeds. Every idle word was the fruit of a dominant attitude.

VI

The foundation attitude of Jesus' life was religious trust. He adventured in the realm of the impracticable because he believed in the power of the living God whom he represented. His life was constantly filled with decisions in which, despite their foreseen consequences, he followed his own principles because he believed that they embodied the will of the Father. To disregard this childlike faith in God is to misunderstand Jesus. To take from his ethical teachings his

[37] Matt. 6:25-34.   [38] Lk. 14:25-35; 9:57-62.

call to religious trust is to denature them. The Fourth
Gospel is a commentary upon this attitude of Jesus.
He had overcome the world even as he faced crucifixion.
He could give his disciples likewise a power of victory
which was very different from that which the world
gave. The unity which he had with his Father was
like the unity which they might have. Whoever
entered the kingdom of God had to be born of the
spirit. Heroic sacrifice born of implicit trust in the
love of a Heavenly Father must be made habitual.

All this Jesus exemplified. He did not recklessly seek
danger; when possible he avoided it.[39] But when it
lay in the path of duty, or when it had to be faced if
love were to be expressed, he never shunned it.[40] He
who called upon men to value loyalty to his ideals
above their own lives did not hesitate to die rather
than abandon his trust in the guidance of a loving
Father.[41]

In death, as in life, he dramatized his teaching.

[39] Lk. 4:28-30.   [40] Jn. 11:7-10; Lk. 13:31-35.   [41] Mk. 10:35-45.

V.

JESUS ON THE FAMILY

ALTHOUGH Jesus taught that the attitude demanded by preparation for the kingdom of God was to be expressed in the family, so far as we can discover the hope of the Jews for the approaching new Age did not concern the family as an institution. There was in the time of Jesus wide discussion of family relations among the rabbinical teachers, but these are mostly concerned with the position of women in society, marriage and divorce, and the proper relation of the sexes. Their messianic hope contains nothing that would argue any difference in marital relations in the coming empire to be established by God other than were involved in the change from one sort of body to another, and even in this regard it did not break with conventional patterns. Jesus, therefore, was under no necessity of opposing asceticism or any tendency toward free love. Such of his teaching on this subject which was not suggested by specific incidents is general in character and part of his exposition of the quality of life which must be possessed by those who would enter the kingdom of God. It was directed to those who were members of his community as the logical exposition of the attitude of love which they could be expected to possess.

I

Marriage, Jesus held, had a divine origin. Husband and wife are joined together by God, so that they are

no longer two but one. It is noteworthy that Jesus
thus regards marriage as monogamous—not indeed
as the result of an evolving conventionality, but as
the result of a divine creative act.[1] Monogamy is
thus regarded by him as the only normal, the only
divine basis of family relations. By this reaffirma-
tion of the noble social teachings of Moses,[2] Jesus
sets his disapproval upon all forms of plural marriage, whether illegal or legal, as violation of the divine
fiat.

But it would be an incomplete presentation of the
position of Jesus to stop at this point. Marriage is
thus ideally not the creature of law. Law can simply
recognize and protect it. With Jesus on its physical
side marriage is an actual union of complementing personalities—a forming of one flesh. It is one of the
primal *facts* of human life, and because it is a conditioning fact and not a merely formal conception of
the lawbooks, it is sacred and inviolable.

On its physical side Jesus regards marriage—like
the other physical elements in the evolving social order
—as an institution to be found only in the present aeon.
The much-married woman of the Sadducees' question[3]
in the life beyond the grave was no longer to be subject
to the perplexing levirate law, for in the resurrection
humanity neither marries nor is given in marriage, but
is to be as the angels of heaven. And yet while Jesus
thus recognizes the physical basis of marriage, he never
speaks of it as sinful or ignoble; so far is he removed
from the perversions that an ascetic faith has so fre-

[1] Matt. 19:5, 6; Mk. 10:6-8.
[2] It should not be overlooked that in using the expression "twain"
Jesus follows the Septuagint rather than the Hebrew, which reads
simply "them." The rabbis made similar use of this passage (Moore,
Judaism, II, 119).
[3] Matt. 22:23-30; Mk. 12:18-25; Lk. 20:27-36.

quently forced upon humanity.[4] As long as human
nature and human relations are as they are, so long will
marriage be the first human tie. But it is altogether
within the spirit of Jesus' teaching to say that the
physical is not the only, nor by any means the permanent element in marriage. This must be found in the
fraternal spirit which guarantees participation in the
coming kingdom. If love is to be supreme between
man and wife there is a union in spirit that springs
from more than sex. The moral union of persons must
accompany the physical. The love and union of husband and wife is like the love and union of children
of a common Father.

It is unnecessary for the appreciation of this position of Jesus to follow him in his terminology. It is of
little or no consequence whether the basis of this conception of the marriage relation be regarded as a literal
divine word or as human nature itself; whether the
institution itself be the outcome of a creative *fiat* or of
evolution. The one essential point is the implication
that the family is a moral unit rather than a mere
legitimizing of sexual relations. It is the molecule of
moral fellowship. Not highly developed animals, but
human personalities form a home.

II

Although marriage is thus sacred, yet some men are
not to marry. Membership in the kingdom of God is
superior. Love will sacrifice a good thing for a better
thing. No man, unless like Origen he be utterly
blinded by an ascetic and fanatic fervor, could ever
misinterpret the intense words in which Jesus expresses

[4] Nor is there a hint of the later Christian teaching that it is
unwise for a widow or widower to remarry.

this axiom. While marriage is good, yet if for any cause it stand in the way of accepting the blessings of the kingdom of heaven, it is to be avoided. Translated into practical morals, this is a call for special self-sacrifice for an ideal on the part of some. The welfare of others, the advancement of society may require the individual to yield private rights. Whether it be to avoid the propagation of an hereditary disease or criminal proclivity, or whether it be that some great mission in life may be the better fulfilled, celibacy may often be the only form of life love would lead a man to adopt. But Jesus does not teach that the men who have thus "made themselves eunuchs for the kingdom of heaven's sake" [5] are holier than men who have sacrificed other individual desires and goods for the common weal. They have their own way of expressing a love that is more than sex. The words of Jesus are a restatement of the familiar teaching of the sacrificed eye and hand.[6] And Jesus himself lived by this standard, a celibate but not an ascetic.

III

The teaching of Jesus regarding divorce is equally absolute. As marriage is one expression of the fundamental moral nature of man, and as it must express the unmodified love which is the human counterpart of the divine goodwill, in theory and as an ideal it is unbreakable. Divorce is regarded by Jesus as impossible for those who have accepted his attitude of love as the law of life. Jesus here was in contrast with his own times and the sex-philosophy of ours. The astonishing laxity which prevailed among the fashionable clique at Rome, even if all due allowance be made for the natural exaggeration of moralists and poets, is well

[5] Matt. 19:12.   [6] Matt. 5:29, 30.

known from the literature of the Empire,[7] to say nothing of the early Christian writers.[8] But the same
tendencies were at work among the less corrupt circles
of Judea. There, too, the general laxity in regard to
divorce was quite as striking. The liberal school of
Hillel was here more the offender than that of Sham-
mai. By an exceedingly broad interpretation of Deut.
24:1 (the sole ground for divorce in the Mosaic code),
it was judged permissible to divorce a wife if she had
spoiled her husband's dinner, and later, if we are to
accept the words of R. Akiba, even if the husband discovered a woman more to his liking.[9] Jesus was in fact
opposed by his countrymen, to whom, thanks to the
popular teaching, his doctrine seemed fanaticism.
Moses, they objected,[10] had allowed divorce, had even
provided that a "bill of divorcement" should be given
in case of separation. Jesus was not to be shaken from
his position by any quotation of ancient authorities.
He admitted that Moses had allowed divorce as an
expedient, a choice between two evils, but, appealing
not to statute but to life, he protested in words his
hearers would have regarded as older even than the law
of Moses, that such permission was in violation of love.
The true children of the kingdom would never avail
themselves of it. All violations of the family union
testify to the failure to embody the attitude of true
love.

It is indicative of the importance Jesus accorded

[7] See Friedländer, *Sittengeschichte der Römer*, I, ch. v; Döllin-
ger, *The Gentile and the Jew*, II, 230*sq*.
[8] See, for instance, Clement of Alexandria and Jerome.
[9] But there is here opportunity, as in the case of Juvenal, for a
large allowance for rhetoric. Yet the general ease of divorce is
undeniable. The Talmud devotes an entire tractate (*Gittin*) to
the subject. See Edersheim, *Life of Jesus the Messiah*, II, 332*sq.;*
Stern, *Die Frau im Talmud;* Weill, *La Femme Juive;* Moore,
Judaism, II, 119-40.
[10] Matt. 19:7.

the family that, not content with thus enunciating a general principle, he should have drawn its corollaries. His position upon many subjects which are of burning interest to-day, and, to judge from the writings of the time, were often quite as much so in his own day, is often noncommittal, almost always reserved, although occasionally, as in the case of ceremonial uncleanness, he expresses in a pregnant sentence a specific principle.[11] But in the matter of divorce he has left us some of the most explicit teaching the gospels have preserved. Under no circumstances is a husband to divorce his wife, or a wife her husband.[12] A husband who puts his wife away, be it never so legally, causes her to be judged as belonging to that class of women who have really given grounds for divorce; he brands her as an adulteress.[13] If on the basis of such divorce she should marry, both she and the new husband commit sin. And similarly in the case of the wife. The original union is still existent.[14] It is evident that

[11] Mk. 7:14, 15.

[12] This addition is noteworthy. It had not been customary among the Jews for wives to divorce their husbands, although about the time of Jesus we meet several cases of its occurrence among the official class. Thus Salome, sister of Herod I divorced her husband (Josephus, *Ant.* xv, 7:10), and later Herodias, at least nominally, divorced her husband Herod, in order to live with his brother, Herod Antipas. The Mishna also grants the wife the right of seeking divorce (*Yebumoth,* 65, a. b. *Cettubboth,* 77, a.). But the custom was more Roman than Jewish.

[13] Matt. 5:32.

[14] This view disregards the exceptive clause in Matt. 5:32 and 19:9. It does not appear in Mk. 10:11, and is also lacking in Lk. 16:18. Wendt (*Teaching of Jesus* I, 354) correctly judges this omission as sufficient ground for the view that "the simple, unqualified statement 'to put away a wife on the ground of unchastity is not culpable adultery,' does not correspond with the meaning of Jesus." That meaning is "that the obligation of marriage is absolute, and no dissolution of it is possible without incurring the guilt of adultery." On critical grounds the addition of the clause by Matthew (so Bleek, Weiss, Holtzmann, and others) is more probable than its omission by Mark. See Hovey, *The Scriptural Law*

Jesus does not command a divorce even in the most extreme cases. It lies outside his ideals. Brotherhood and the need of reconciliation would certainly favor a maintenance of old relations even after divorce is legally permissible. Forgiveness and reconciliation are as much the supreme needs in the family as at the altar.[15]

The ground for this definite deduction is not hard to discover. It is a corollary of the absolute ideal of those who are like their Heavenly Father. His teaching is intended for those aspiring souls who call him Master.

Marriage, both in its lower and its higher aspects, is the basis of family unity. Family life is the most sacred of all relations outside of the relation between God and man. It is not to be violated even in look and thought. Adultery may be committed even when lust never passes beyond the licentious glance.[16] In proportion as the natural sanctity of marriage is injured, in the same proportion is the nature of man outraged and ideal fraternity broken. To dishonor this first of human relationships is to loosen the bonds of society, to lower social ideals, and is inconsistent with

of Divorce, and Studies in Ethics and Religion, 321sq., and commentaries (especially Meyer, and Broadus) on the above passages. See also Strong, Philosophy and Religion, 431-442, and Woolsey, Divorce and Divorce Legislation, ch. ii, although so far as his interpretation of the teaching of Jesus on this point is concerned, President Woolsey's views were later reversed. (See the essay by President Strong just mentioned.) The Roman church has not favored divorce of a freely entered and ecclesiastically regular marriage except for marital unfaithfulness. See Schmidt, Social Results of Christianity, 201sq., and, especially for the Roman Catholic position, Convers, Marriage and Divorce, and Pascal, "L'Association Catholique," Revue des Questions Sociales et Ouvrieres, January, 1896. Peabody, Jesus Christ and the Social Question, 150sq. has a characteristically sane discussion of the entire matter.

[15] Matt. 5:23, 24.
[16] Matt. 5:27, 28.

the love that should characterize husband and wife. It was, therefore, not in the spirit of a purist or a fanatic that Jesus thus put checks upon divorce, but because of his own central attitude. It was the underlying principles of this attitude that led him in the face of popular opinion thus to formulate for the group of his intimate followers the rigid application of love to human relationship.

IV

Modern sentiment, like the legislation and the sentiment of the professional teachers of Jesus' day, is opposed to treating marriage as an aspect of the strictly moral life. Marriage is assuming much more the character of a legal status than of a natural union. Its continuance is increasingly believed to be dependent upon the desires of the parties concerned and the decision of the courts.

It has never been possible in legislation to assume Jesus' ideal of absolute and perfect love between husband and wife. This Jesus himself recognized. Divorce had been permitted by Moses because of the hardness of his people's hearts. But Jesus was not a legislator dealing with society at large, but an expounder of attitudes for the group preparing for the kingdom. The attempts to prevent divorce in human society, even with the exception of cases of marital unfaithfulness, have never been successful. In fact, they seem to have tended toward the increase of illegitimacy. Even when marriage has been wholly an affair of the church the absolute prohibition of divorce has not conduced unqualifiedly to the welfare of society. If we could assume that all persons were possessed of the attitude

of Jesus and that they were as wise as they were loving, the question of divorce would of course not emerge.
But such a presupposition is contrary to reality. The
family is only a partially christianized institution.
Society has always abounded and still abounds with
persons whose lives are far enough removed from complete consecration to the ideals of Jesus. It is dangerous to legislate as if the case were otherwise. Just
as human experience has shown it to be inevitable
that the state must regulate the relation of the sexes
in the interests of public morality, so it has become
inevitable that the principle of love must find its legislative expression in the choice of the less of two evils
that beset a social institution. Family life unfortu-
nately is no more completely subject to the ideals of
Jesus than is any other social institution. His
ideal cannot be administered legally without causing
vast suffering and in some cases imperiling and even
wrecking the stability of the social order. Herein the
point of view of legislation must always be different
from that of Jesus, for it must recognize development
in general morality. It certainly is more in accordance
with the principle of love and the giving of justice
to end a marriage in which either husband or wife
suffers from the wrongdoing, not to say brutality, of
the other than to insist that the two shall live together
without such release. It is the duty of love to protect
the victims of evil persons.

It is, of course, lamentable that this is the case,
but it would be even more lamentable and dangerous to
deny that it is the case. So long as men and women
are imperfect, the desire to give justice must recognize
the necessity of an approach to an ideal rather than

of an attempt to force people without ideals to live as if they possessed them. The practical question concerns the wisdom of any legislative attempt to control such loveless lives.

It does not need to be added that such an expression of love as finding imperfect, but it is to be hoped, progressive social expression in remedial and preventive measures implies no approval of hasty divorce or hasty marriage. The central consideration is not that of the relation of the sexes but of the home as an institution. Too much modern discussion of marriage fails to make this distinction. Any proposal to palliate indiscriminate sexual unions by some new terminology is to ignore the fact that marriage is intended as the first step in the setting up of a social institution. It is at this point that the teaching of Jesus gains a new moral application. If human beings are to make biological considerations primary they are not fully realizing their significance as persons. For such an estimate of human beings Jesus cannot be quoted, nor can there be any compromise or adjustment of his teaching. The very center of his teaching is to the contrary. And in the same proportion as individuals order their lives in accordance with the personal values which his teachings of love imply, the institution of the family gains in permanence and personal value. The family is a moral institution. Any psychology that would reduce human life to the level of its animal origin is contrary not only to the teachings of Jesus as regards love, but to the significance of that process which we call evolution. To attempt to cheapen the family by treating it as if it were not based on personality is to run counter to the tendency of the age-long experience of struggle and hope which has brought social life away from its early animal stages to its present complicated and more personal character.

What is this experience ·but a signpost pointing to the ideal of Jesus? If all families embodied the love of the Heavenly Father, who would think of divorce or of sexual irregularity?

VI.

JESUS ON WEALTH

JESUS was not a teacher of political economy, but he was not indifferent to economic affairs. His followers were drawn almost entirely from the unprivileged class. In fact, it was their poverty that gave rise to their revolutionary hopes. They felt the political oppression of Rome, but they also knew the pressure of need. As they looked forward to the better day which was to come, they saw harvests of grain and limitless supplies of wine.[1] The poor are naturally hostile to the rich, and this hostility was to be found in the masses of Palestine to which Jesus appealed.

I

His sympathy with the poor colored the teaching of Jesus. He was not dealing with problems of industry or commerce, of international trade or economic theory, but he was a friend of the dispossessed.

But at this point the interpreter must be loyal to his method. There have been those who could see in Jesus a class-conscious agitator.[2] To them he is a carpenter who attempted proletarian leadership. Since he was killed by the authorities and the well-to-do, he

[1] See Enoch 10:20-22. Curiously enough Papias records an alleged saying of Jesus to this effect.
[2] Bouck White, *The Call of the Carpenter;* Kalthoff, *Das Leben Jesus,* and socialist interpreters of Jesus.

becomes a martyr of the working classes and his death a sacrament of class hatred.

There is an element of justice in this conception of Jesus. He certainly did gather the masses about himself, and he certainly did warn his disciples against wealth. He saw that the well-fed and the well-clothed were in the houses of the rich.[3] He repeatedly uses some aspect of property for illustration, yet all but invariably in such a way as to give the impression that he could see in wealth a source of arbitrary and dangerous power. In fact, there seems to have been nothing, unless it be hypocrisy, which appeared to Jesus so full of danger as wealth.

To the student of revolutions there is nothing peculiar in enmity toward the more privileged, and Jesus would be by no means unique if his sympathies with the crowds who listened to him had led him to appeal to cupidity and class consciousness. Here, as in the field of politics, the road to successful demagogism lay open. He had only to inflame the passions of his followers to have led a peasants' revolt. In the development of economic class consciousness, full of danger to the prosperous classes, Jesus might have found a cause even more appealing than that of armed revolt. There would have been a possibility, at least, that readjustments might have been made in taxes or that better administration would have been given agriculture and the fishing industry. There were not lacking precedents in which political authorities had so acted. In such an effort to get new economic rights for his people he might have won the reputation of a safe and sane reformer.

But he turned from all appeals to hatred to the insistence on goodwill.

[3] Lk. 7:24, 25.

True, misinterpretation is here easy. In many of his sayings Jesus discriminates harshly against the rich. To the rich, to the well-fed, to the merry, is foretold woe.[4] "It is easier," he once said, after he had seen an earnest, rich young man turn from him, "for a camel to go through a needle's eye than for a rich man to enter into the kingdom of heaven."[5] In the most awful of his parables he portrays the beggar Lazarus as sharing in the joys of the blessed, unable to carry the least of his comforts to the rich man suffering torments across the great gulf.[6] Our one monument of non-Pauline Christianity is full of this severity.[7] It seems but the corollary of this discrimination when Jesus called upon his disciples to share their wealth with the poor. Such of them as had property were bidden to sell it and to give alms,[8] and no one who asked for aid was to be denied. The young man who had lived an exemplary life from his youth was told that if he would be perfect he should sell what he had and give to the poor.[9] Nay, even if one had his goods taken from him he was not to seek them again.[10] And charity was not only to be extended, it was to be enjoyed. When Jesus first sent out the Twelve and (according to Luke) subsequently the Seventy, among other directions he gave them was that they take no money and accept hospitality from all whom they deemed worthy.[11] Within the immediate circle of his friends the same principle to some extent held good,

---

[4] Lk. 6:24. There is a critical possibility that these words are not those of Jesus himself, but it is supported by arguments so purely subjective as to render conviction difficult.

[5] Matt. 18:24.

[6] Lk. 16:19-31.

[7] James 1:10, 11; 2:1-7; 4:13; 5:1-6.

[8] Lk. 12:33.

[9] Matt. 19:16-22.

[10] Matt. 5:42.

[11] Lk. 10:5-7.

for not only did Jesus apparently give to the poor,[12] but he himself was supported, at least in part, by devoted women.[13] For Jesus was a poor man without home of his own,[14] and dependent upon others not only for support but for that hospitality which his own kinsmen seemed to have refused or so to have offered as to have made its acceptance a confession of insanity.[15]

From one of these cases it appears that the renunciation of wealth was one of the conditions of joining the new society. But it is not without parallels. The fishers of the lake were called to leave a prosperous business to become fishers of men.[16] Matthew left his *octroi* station near Capernaum [17] to follow Jesus, and even the money-changers of the Temple saw their tables overturned and their fellow monopolists fleeing before the Galilean who had found his Father's house made into a den of thieves.[18]

It would not be at all strange, therefore, if from these teachings and facts men should have concluded that the pursuit of wealth was unchristian and wealth itself an evil rather than a good. And so men have thought in all times since the days of Jesus. The preaching of the church against wealth has been equaled only by its zeal to obtain it. Those early ascetics who saw in the body only evil, and who sought with Simon of the Pillar to please God by the hideous mortification of the flesh, have been far outnumbered by the multitude of men who have by vows of poverty as well as celibacy endeavored to make themselves acceptable in the eyes of God. Few have so far imi-

[12] Jn. 13:29.   [15] Mk. 3:21.
[13] Lk. 8:3.   [16] Mk. 1:16, 17; Matt. 4:18, 19.
[14] Matt. 8:19, 20; Lk. 9, 57, 58.   [17] Matt. 8:9.
[18] Mk. 11:17; Matt. 21:17; Lk. 19:46.

tated St. Francis as to strip off wealth and clothes alike
and start at the new birth as naked as the new babe,
but every religious revival of the Middle Ages blos-
somed into fresh devotions of wealth to order or church
and of life to the sanctifying processes of want.
Through the centuries in which the leaven of Jesus
has been working in society, wealth has enormously
increased, but the processes of distribution have not
developed so rapidly as those of production. The poor
have been always present, and the Christian church
has always endeavored, with more or less wisdom, to
do them good.[19] They are God's poor. But too seldom
has such benefaction perfectly represented Jesus, and
too often has it hindered the realization of his more
fundamental principles in economic processes. The
ethics of production have sometimes been obscured by
the charity of the exploiters of men. Charity has for
centuries been too often the palliative of sin and the
deadener of conscience. If patriotism has been once
the last refuge of a scoundrel, charity has been a
thousand times the hypocrite's bid for heaven.

It is, however, only the superficial elements in his
life that really make Jesus appear a proletarian leader.
He ceased to be a carpenter when he became the
Master. His interest was not in economics but in persons. Men could enjoy higher values than wealth.
Covetousness on the part of a poor man was as evil
as on the part of a rich man.[20] His own poverty was
obvious but he did not make it a basis of appeal to
popular sympathy. He lived on charity, but he never
declaimed against his lot. His view of wealth is not
to be found in this or that particular saying, but in

[19] See, for instance, Uhlhorn, *Christian Charity in the Early
Church;* Harnack, *The Expansion of Christianity,* I, 181-249.
[20] Lk. 12:13-15.

the entire scope and course of his life and teachings.
We do for Jesus simply what we do for every teacher
whose method was like his, if we attempt to discover
an attitude which underlies and a principle that binds
together all specific sayings.

II

How far Jesus was from to-day's interests in economic matters appears in his absolute silence regarding
the problems connected with the production of wealth.
In part this may have been due to the existence of
slavery, but Jesus says nothing about the emancipation
of slaves. It may have been due partly to the absence
of anything like the present capitalist organization
of society, but Jesus has nothing to say about the
moral aspects of trade. In fact, when he refers to economic matters either directly or by way of illustration,
his language is that of the small-town artisan. Even
where he uses the wage scale as an illustration, it is
to the purport that the employer in giving wages has
a right to do as he will with his own.[21] To attempt to
derive from this parable any teaching for our elaborate
economic system would be worse than futile. It is far
wiser to recognize frankly the fact that just as Jesus'
teaching is nonpolitical, so is it in any strict sense of
the term, noneconomic. How fortunate this is appears
when one recalls how inappropriate teachings applicable to the agricultural and commercial world of his
day might be to an industrial age like ours.

When we undertake to estimate the teaching of
Jesus from the point of view of his immediate surroundings, we can see that his real purpose is to set
forth the meaning of goodwill. His interest is not in

[21] Matt. 20:1-16.

wealth, but in human possibilities. The attitude of goodwill, upon which he relies because of its accord with the goodwill of God, will find different expressions in different economic situations. But whatever the nature of the economic society, the moral principle and motive which Jesus emphasizes will be the same. Its expression will differ in accordance with men's perception of particular needs.[22]

This general principle is clear: the economic life must be dominated by brotherliness. Wealth must be gained and used for the benefit of others as well as for oneself. It should not be governed by mere acquisitiveness. Jesus gave an extreme illustration of this. A landowner's agent [23] by trickiness won friends for himself by appealing to their cupidity. In fact, having reduced their rentals dishonestly, he could expect to live permanently on blackmail. Jesus pointed out that this was far-sightedness on the part of dishonest people. Money could be used to make friends. So it might be used by honest people. Men were to make friends with the Mammon of unrighteousness that when wealth itself failed these friends might receive their benefactor into "eternal habitation." But Jesus did not let the matter stop there. The use of money is a test of character. For if a man be unfaithful in the affairs of business, Jesus regards him as liable to be unfaithful in matters of greater importance.[24] The rich man suffering in torments had a thought of his brothers too late, and his wealth had made no friends.

[22] Heuver, *The Teaching of Jesus Concerning Wealth;* Rogge, *Der irdische Besitz im N. T.;* Cone, *Rich and Poor in the N. T.*

[23] Lk. 16:1-13.

[24] Lk. 16:10, 12. Clement of Alexandria, in his little tract *The Salvation of Rich Men,* puts this admirably: "Earthly property should be considered in the light of a staff, an instrument for good uses."

He had served Mammon, but not God. So, too, Jesus condemned [25] the rich fool who, after he had accumulated wealth, planned to use it selfishly for his own enjoyment. In the genuine epicurean call to his soul, "Thou hast much goods laid up for thyself; eat, drink, and be merry," this man published his determination to avoid all the possibilities of benefiting society wealth put in his hands. Wealth is therefore a desirable good only so far as it is a means to a man's highest development—that is, only so long as it renders him more capable of fulfilling Jesus' ideal of fraternity. For as Jesus pertinently asked, "What shall it profit a man if he gain the whole world and yet lose himself?" [26] A man's heart will be with his treasure, and there is more lasting wealth than silver and gold.[27]

It is against this danger which lies within acquisitiveness that Jesus especially warns his followers. It is a simple matter of observation that, instead of increasing a man's social sympathies, the struggle for fortune too often makes him selfish and unsocial in that it breaks down that sense of dependence which the poor man feels binding him to other men. In the same proportion as the semblance of independence increases is there danger that a man will forget that he is always an integral part of society and that he can be truly a person only as he is in sympathy with his fellows. This was the trouble evidently enough with the rich young man of whom we have already spoken. He was endeavoring to build up a perfection upon the cornerstone of a selfish individualism. This is the secret of Jesus' command to trust the Heavenly Father for clothes and food.[28] These things are not evil, but

[25] Lk. 12:16-21.   [26] Lk. 9:25.   [27] Matt. 6:19-21.
[28] Matt. 6:31-33. See also his warning against covetousness, Lk. 12:15.

if once regarded as the highest good they will inevitably lead to a selfish competition for personal advantage at the cost of generous impulses and faith.

With such a conception of the application of good-will to the economic life, Jesus could consistently be only severe in his condemnation of whatever makes against brotherliness. No man ever had a deeper sympathy with the poor and unfortunate. Like them, he felt profoundly the misery and injustice which spring from the irresponsible power of the wealthy, and sought with all his strength to arouse new feelings of the need of giving justice. Yet he was the farthest possible from economic fanaticism. He himself was able to live with poor and rich alike.[29] If he was homeless, the houses of the rich were often at his service. If his head was sometimes wet with the dews of heaven, he knew also what it was to have poured upon him costly ointment. He welcomed the rich Zacchaeus quite as heartily as his fellow citizen, the beggar Bartimaeus. Where is there more business optimism than in his advice to lend money to those in need, never despairing of its repayment?[30] Indeed, his life expresses even more distinctly than his words the coördination of his teachings.

All the more weighty, therefore, is his judgment upon the unworthy rich. Wealth he showed to be a

[29] It is a mistake to think of early Christians as altogether from the poorest classes. They were from the well-to-do and even wealthy classes as well, as appears not only from the Acts and certain allusions in the epistles, but also from evidence furnished by the Catacombs. So far is it from being true that Christianity was a proletarian movement. See Rosse, *La Roma Sotteranea Cristiana;* Northcote and Brownlow, *Roma Sotteranea.*

[30] Lk. 6:35. The Authorized Version completely abscures the thought of Jesus by its arbitrary mistranslation of ἀπελπίζοντες. Yet it is hardly historical to plead that Jesus intended to be a good adviser for business men. Cf. Barton, *The Man Nobody Knows.*

good, but only when it is a social good and when its pursuit does not weaken those impulses within a man that go out toward his fellows and God. Then he becomes unfit for the kingdom of heaven. Inevitable and fearful punishment awaited the man whose wealth brought no joy to others than himself.

III

All this, it must be admitted, brings Jesus close to the general position of socialism. If the attitude of love would make economic goods not means of purely individual enjoyment but consecrated to the good of society, and if the ideal society is a brotherhood, it is not a long step to the belief that any form of private property is anti-fraternal and that society itself can best administer economic matters for the good of its members. Something like corroboration is given such an interpretation of Jesus' position by the fact that the company of his followers had a common purse,[31] and that the members of the primitive Jerusalem church "had all things in common."[32]

It is therefore by no means strange that there have always been those who have maintained that in some

[31] Jn. 12:19; 13;6. These texts are so used by Todt, *Der radikale deutsche Socialismus.*

[32] Acts 2:44, 45; 4:32, 36, 37. It is just here that unrhetorical describtion seems almost beyond hope. For instance, Leslie Stephen (*Social Rights and Duties,* I, 21, 22): "The early Christians were the socialists of their age, and took a view of Dives and Lazarus which would commend itself to the Nihilists of to-day . . . if the man who best represents the ideas of early Christians were to enter a respectable society of to-day, would it not be likely to send for the police?" A master of clever English like Leslie Stephen has small need of such astonishing nonsense as this to get himself a hearing. Laveleye (*Primitive Property,* Intro. xxxi.), though writing in a different spirit, makes an equally indefensible statement: "If Christianity were taught and understood conformably to the spirit of its Founder, the existing social organism could not last a day."

form of socialism lay the true program of Christianity. It has repeatedly happened that a revival of faith and zeal has been accompanied by some doctrine as to community of goods. "If there were no sin, all temporal goods would be held in common" has been the cry of more than one Raymund Lull. To a considerable degree this is seen beneath the policy of the great medieval monastic orders and of ultra-reformers like some of the Anabaptists. But in most of these cases their limited communism has been accompanied by more or less asceticism to which the spirit of modern socialism is radically opposed. No man, however, can bring any such charge against the Christian socialists of England, Germany, or America. The great inducement to combine Christianity and socialism lies along the very different line of their professed search for greater happiness and completeness in life, and it cannot be denied that the combination has great attractions. Indeed, if socialism be only what Maurice [33] declared it to be, "the acknowledgment of brotherhood and fellowship in work," it is but a phase of Christianity.

To think of Jesus as gentle idealist who preached a communism which was neither coarse nor practicable; to see in the Jerusalem church a group of kindred idealists attempting to practice the same unworldly economy; to see only sophistry in the word of any man who ventures to think that the early church fathers did not regard riches as the fruit of usurpation —all this is captivating, but it will hardly bear severe scrutiny. [34]

[33] *Life,* II, 128.
[34] So Nitti, *Le Socialisme Catholique,* especially chs. ii, iii. Less learned but equally extreme views are constantly to be met. For instance, R. Heber Newton, *Social Studies,* 332sq. It is gratify-

For it is futile to attempt to discover modern socialism in the words of Jesus. There is, it is true, nothing
incompatible with such a system were it once proved
to be the means best adapted to furthering the true
spirit of brotherliness; but this is just as true of a
rational individualism. The follower of Jesus must
sympathize heartily with those who denounce grind-
ing competition or a supposed "iron law of wages," but
as a follower of Jesus one stands committed to neither
socialism nor individualism. Before either is declared
unchristian it must be shown to be hopelessly opposed
to goodwill. Charity, with Jesus, is not communism.
If it could be proved that he had been an Essene, the
identification might be easier, but that possibility is
now little thought of.[35] Probably no one would soberly
commit Jesus to communism because of Judas and
the bag, and so far as any direct word or single act of
his is concerned, it is necessary to say the same. Even
in the case of the primitive Jerusalem church it is
impossible to discover anything like communism in the
modern sense of the word. Its members, be they never
so rich, were not required to sell their possessions and
to give to the poor, if we are to accept the words of
Peter to Ananias.[36] Indeed, the story of Ananias and
Sapphira does not make their fate dependent upon
their failure to share all their property, but upon their
lying to the effect that they had so done. Nor does it

ing to find an opposite view presented in so important a work as
Nathusius, *Die Mitarbeit der Kirche an der Lösung der Socialen
Frage*, II, 274*sq.* As one would expect, thorough historians reject
the idea of there having been communism in the Jerusalem church,
for instance, Weizsäcker, *History of the Apostolic Age* (Eng. ed.), I,
56. See also Keim, *Jesus of Nazara*, III, 345-347.

[35] See Godet, *Commentary on Luke;* Lightfoot, *Commentary on
the Epistle to the Colossians*, Appendix; Renan, *History of the
People of Israel*, V, 48-66.

[36] Acts 4:4.

appear that all the members of the church at Jerusalem disposed of their property, since the mother of Mark had her own house.[37]   As a matter of fact, it would seem that this sharing of wealth in Jerusalem was simply an expression of natural enthusiasm and Christian love. It may, perhaps, have involved a too literal interpretation of Jesus' words, but even this is by no means clear. At any rate, a few years after this so-called communism we find the church at Jerusalem counseling, not communism, but generosity to the poor,[38] and Paul's effort to raise a "contribution for the poor among the saints in Jerusalem" replacing the "having of things in common." [39]   If there really had ever been any communism, its outcome was a *reductio ad absurdum*—a commentary upon the need of care in using the words of Jesus that will repay reflection.[40]

In the matter of charity we find Jesus expressing by his life the common sense that is to be used in the interpretation of his more radical statements. When his friends saw fit to criticize a woman who had anointed him, on the ground that the cost of the ointment might much better have been given to the poor, Jesus rebukes them, though using those words which so often have incited to charity, "The poor ye have with you always, that when ye will ye may do them good." [41]   There was a duty higher than charity. It

---

[37] Acts 12:12.   [38] Gal. 2:9.   [39] Rom. 15:26.

[40] What means would be left of communicating one to another, if none had the means to bestow" (i.e., had given everything away)? asks Clement of Alexandria, who doubtless saw that the Christians of Alexandria needed little encouragement to engage in business if the words of the Emperor Hadrian to his brother-in-law, Servianus, are correct. Speaking of the inhabitants of Alexandria he says, "They have all of them but one God—money; 'tis he alone that Christians, Jews, and all the rest adore."

[41] Matt. 26: 6-11.

would, indeed, be far less correct to say that Jesus taught indiscriminate giving than to say that, according to his general principle of love, charity may at times be forbidden as hurtful rather than helpful.

IV

The application to modern economic conditions of this teaching of Jesus regarding brotherhood is difficult only when we treat his words as those of one seeking to organize economic life. Then they become impracticable. His unsparing denunciation of those who build life upon acquisitiveness becomes an attack upon wealth itself. His sympathy for the oppressed people of his own day becomes justification of hostility to our existing social order. His merciless portrayal of the outcome of the spirit of the rich man who would let Lazarus rot among the dogs becomes a justification of an assault upon all rich men. But this is to misinterpret Jesus and to use his name in vain—to make him an economist when he is a herald of a moral attitude.

It is clear that no human society with which we have any acquaintance was ever built or could ever be built on disregard of economic goods. Poor peoples have little art, little education, few public institutions.

Unless progress from primitive savagery to our present civilization be regarded as degenerate, wealth must be recognized as one basis for such progress. To insist that every man with Jesus' ideals of service must give all his property away is not only to put a premium on beggary, but it is to put economic power exclusively in the hands of those who, repudiating his teaching as to love, are unqualifiedly acquisitive. As celibacy in the name of religion tended to breed out the more spiritually minded from the European stock, so a religious pursuit of poverty would tend to breed out the possibility of controlling economic life by Christian ideals.

The question, therefore, whether Jesus has any meaning for an economically developing social order is not to be answered by erecting epigrams into laws. If he is to have influence in the economic world, we must eliminate from his teaching elements which obviously arose from his expectation of the speedy coming of the kingdom and the end of time. Chief among these removals would be his teachings as to the giving away of wealth as a universal prerequisite of entering into the joys of the kingdom, as well as the command that his followers sell what they had and give to the poor. Such directions are intelligible if Jesus thought that the world would soon come to an end, but they can never be used as determining factors in the economic life of his followers. The problems of production are unmentioned by him.

We must not treat his immediate relations with a discontented, oppressed, poverty-stricken people as something to be generalized into a universal ethical ideal. For there is no necessary virtue in poverty any more than there is necessarily evil in wealth. If Jesus had given the slightest intimation that he had an economic theory like that of Karl Marx, his words regarding wealth would, of course, have an entirely new meaning, but he had no economic philosophy and no permanent economic program. His interest in any concrete situation, whether it be marriage or property, is that of one who is endeavoring to get men to see that the basic need in life is the expression of a love like that of the Heavenly Father. Poverty may check

this, wealth may check it. Neither is injurious because
of itself, but because it stimulates the spirit of acquisitiveness and selfishness. In a social order like ours
the consistent Christian will endeavor to base economic processes on a true recognition of personal
values, cease to think of labor as a commodity, and
endeavor to use whatever wealth he has morally
gained in the interest of human welfare.

Acquisitiveness is not limited to those who have
property. It is also the attitude of the unprivileged.
What others have they want. Like the ancient
Hebrews, they pass by cities or vineyards of others
and believe that their God has given such blessings
to them. They believe in brotherhood because they
hope to get something from their brothers. They
believe in justice because they feel that if justice were
done the rich would be cast down and they, poor but
worthy, would be lifted to high estate. When was
there a revolutionary movement in which there was
not a demand for privilege and a determination in
some way to gain it? A declaration of rights is a
precursor of civil war.

Jesus, with his profound sympathy with the masses,
sensed this attitude on the part of his contemporaries
and sought to correct it. And in so doing he rose above
economic programs. Emphasizing solely a moral attitude, Jesus cannot be found to be an economist. He
is neither a champion nor an opponent of *laissez faire;*
he neither forbids trades unions, strikes, and lockouts,
nor advises them; he was neither socialist nor indi-
vidualist. Jesus was a friend neither of the working
man nor the rich man as such. He dealt with persons,
not economic classes. The question he would put to
a man is not "Are you rich?" "Are you poor?" but

"Have you done the will of my Father and loved all men?" The answer to this question must be left to economic wisdom energized by goodwill. The first point to be settled is as to whether an existing economic institution or custom or effort tends to the establishment of fraternity. If it does not, the face of Christ is against it, and the only escape from his woe is to abolish whatever keeps its possessor from using or producing wealth to the advantage of society. For such minds as would regard this as an ethical platitude, Jesus furnishes abundant stimulus in the sayings of the Sermon on the Mount. For those who itch less for sensational novelties, this teaching of Jesus will furnish the point of departure for any economic philosophy that cares to use his name.

VII.

JESUS ON THE STATE

THE emphasis which Jesus placed upon a social attitude rather than upon social legislation is especially evident in his teaching about the state. As has already been pointed out, the revolutionary psychology to which he appealed contained political elements which were at last to break all restraints and involve the Jews repeatedly in fatal conflict with the Romans. Jesus constantly faced the temptation to capitalize these insurrectionary forces. That appears from the story of the temptation and from his words to Peter at the time when his disciples declared their faith in him as their expected messiah.[1] But, as he told Pilate, if the kingdom for which he prepared men had been of this age his followers would have fought.[2] His insistence on the spirit of love as indispensable for those who would enjoy the blessings of God's kingdom made any championship of violence out of the question. His disciples even when prosecuted were not to rely upon force but upon divine help.[3]

I

Jesus was alive to national duties. He was not an internationalist but a Jew with a mission to the lost sheep of the house of Israel. His nation was precious, and he foresaw distinctly the dangers which the revo-

[1] Mk. 8:31-38.   [2] Jn. 18:33-37.   [3] Mk. 13:9, 11-13.

lutionary and military spirit threatened.[4]   Just as
clearly did he recognize its possibilities as a nation of
those who embodied the attitude he saw in God.   His
individualism was therefore not that of the anarchist.
He presented himself dramatically to his capital city
for acceptance as representative of the spirit of the
coming kingdom.[5]   It is no wonder that the people of
Jerusalem who had not seen him since the beginning
of his public career should have been astonished at
the Galileans' saluting him as the Son of David.   But
even his followers were disillusioned as they saw their
Christ weeping over Jerusalem and forecasting its
doom.   For when the little procession of unarmed
men escorting an unarmed and humble Galilean were
asked by the people of Jerusalem who Jesus was, they
replied that he was the prophet of Nazareth.   The
bitterness of his disappointment is easily understood.
He had sought to influence his people to recognize
their mission as the representatives of a rightly conceived God of Israel, but they had ignored his message
and clung to the hope of a national messiah, the Son
of David.   He saw clearly what tragedies this super-
nationalism involved.   The Pharisees might hope to
win the world to God by proselyting, but the insurrectionary, militaristic elements within the state would
bring about the destruction of the city.   And time was
to prove his forecast correct.   His cleansing of the
Temple was the outgrowth of the same desire to arouse
his people to a true mission to the world.   The Temple
that should have been the house of prayer for all
nations had been exploited by the priestly coterie for
their own financial advantage.   With this effort the

[4] Lk. 19:41-44.
[5] This is the meaning of the so-called triumphal entry (Mk. 11:1-11
and parallels).

more spiritually minded Pharisees must have sympathized,[6] but they could not see in Jesus one who had any authority for aggressive reform. It is always difficult for the professional teacher of religion to treat respectfully the nonprofessional. Such drastic action as he took in the Court of the Temple served only to arouse the fear of popular uprising, and as Caiaphas is reported to have said,[7] it seemed better for one man to die than for the nation to suffer at the hands of its political master.

But beyond this attempt to call his nation to its religious opportunity and duty Jesus did not go. He did not deal with the nation as a political unit, and his teaching was no more political than was his action. He was endeavoring to inculcate attitudes in the individual soul rather than to organize a new state or to urge political reform. The revolutionary psychology of his followers had to be purged of hatred and appeal to force. Otherwise the kingdom of heaven would be given to others than Jews.[8]

II

Jesus nowhere gives political teaching. His non-interfering attitude toward the state and political relations is to be seen, in his own life, in scattered statements, and in general comparisons and implications.

As regards his own life, it is evident that he obeyed the local and imperial governments under which he lived, and that he distinctly refused to be made a governor or a king, or in any way to be involved in political revolution, preferring death to political agitation.[9] All this is evident in his transformation of the revo-

---

[6] Herford, *The Pharisees*, ch. iv. [8] Lk. 14:15-24; Matt. 22:1-10.
[7] Jn. 11:49, 50. [9] Jn. 6:15; 18:36; Acts 1:5sq.

lutionary psychology. The most celebrated text,[10] "Render unto Caesar the things that are Caesar's, and unto God the things that are God's," is rather an avoidance of specific teaching than an enunciation of a principle. The position in which Jesus found himself precluded direct answer.[11] That was why his opponents asked the question. His answer, therefore, was one that might be interpreted either favorably or unfavorably according to the conception his opponents held as to whether or not Caesar really owned the coins. Once grant (as the account would lead us to suppose they did grant) that "the image and superscription" on the coin implied the sovereignty of Caesar, and the reply of Jesus would of necessity pronounce the payment of taxes legitimate.[12] Deny that implication and his reply says nothing of the law. It is, therefore, obvious that any wide application of this text to the exigencies of politics must first of all presuppose the sovereign rights of the ruler. Besides, it is clear that in the mind of Jesus the emphasis was upon the thought of rendering to God the things that were his. The entire reply was a rebuke to insidious quibbling and a refusal to be drawn into politics as an excuse for submission to tyranny or as an incentive to a struggle for independence.[13]

[10] Matt. 22:18-22.

[11] The taxes were a constant cause of revolt. See Josephus, *Ant.* xviii, 1:1-6; xx, 5:2; Acts 5:37.

[12] That the effigy was regarded by the Jews as implying sovereignty is clear from the fact in the revolt against Hadrian they restamped the Roman coins. See Madden, *Coins of the Jews,* 176, 203, and Renan, *Life of Jesus* (Am. ed., 1895), 337n.

[13] Matt. 17:27; Renan, *Life of Jesus* (Am. ed., 1895), 338. The tax was not political, but a religious levy for the support of the Temple at Jerusalem. See Edersheim, *Life and Times of Jesus the Messiah,* II, 111-13. See also Ex. 30:11*sq;* Neh. 10:32*sq.* The Mishna has a separate treatise on the subject.

More distinct is the reply of Jesus to the well-meant boast of Pilate [14] that he had the power of punishing or acquitting: "Thou wouldst have no authority against me, except it were given thee from above." At the first glance it might appear as if these words are to be taken according to their historical interpretation and thus commit Jesus to the theory of the divine right of kings, not to mention the whole mass of pusillanimity and casuistry known as the doctrine of Passive Obedience. But it seems strange to think of Jesus at this supreme hour setting forth a political theory. It is much more natural to regard these words as a part of his philosophy of providence.[15] They do indeed recognize Pilate as a judge, and express submission to a government as to any fact of society, but they by no means make the right of kings any more divine than a myriad other rights.

Nor when we pass from the search for definite statements to a consideration of the implications and the comparisons of the teachings of Jesus do we gain any more definite results. He frequently uses certain phases of royal life to illustrate his teachings: the kingdom of God in some respects, he said, was like a would-be king who had rebellious subjects; [16] or a king who gave a marriage supper to his son, only to find himself insulted; [17] or a king who was more merciful than one of his subjects; [18] while the misfortunes that come upon a kingdom torn by civil war furnished him arguments for proving his own innocence of complicity with Satan.[19] These comparisons,

[14] Jn. 19:11.
[15] Compare Matt. 6:25-34.
[16] Lk. 19:11*sq.*
[17] Matt. 22:2.
[18] Matt. 18:23*sq.*
[19] Mk. 3:24; Matt. 12:25*sq.*

coupled with the absence of any serious [20] criticism
of royalty, make it safe to say that, while we are lacking in definite political teaching emanating from Jesus,
we cannot maintain to the contrary that he regarded
government as an evil. But his kingdom was indeed
not of this world,[21] and these comparisons yield no
data for generalization.[22] Even the apostles gave
more political teaching than he.

III

Was Jesus, then, an anarchist?

The question is absurd if one means by anarchy
the philosophy of dynamite and terror. But this, of
course, is only a caricature of a far more tenable political philosophy. Proudhon's "anarchic government"
was to be no more full of violence than the "natural"
state of Rousseau. The name has unfortunate associations, but, at least as the name of a philosophy,
may stand for an ideal condition, which is to be the
expression of law. But this law is no longer, as with
Thomas Aquinas, the outflow of the divine nature,
but is rather the expression of a human nature that
is instinctively to do that which is good not only in
the eyes of its possessor, but also in those of his
neighbors.

"Anarchy is not inconsistent with association, but
only with enforced association. It means simply a

[20] For no one except a fanatic would see in the somewhat cutting
reference to the luxury of courts (Matt. 11:8; Lk. 7:25) anything
opposed to monarchy as such. Nor do the references to trials before
kings and judges (Matt. 10:18) imply any opposition to the institutions they represent.
[21] Jn. 18:36.
[22] Simkovitch, *Toward the Understanding of Jesus*, finds a warning against political revolt in the sayings concerning nonresistance.
Such an implication is plausible but fails to recognize the central,
nonpolitical purpose of Jesus.

state of society in which no one is bound or obliged
to do anything (whether to associate with others or
anything else); it is not opposed to order, but only
to enforced order; nor to rule, but only to obligatory
rule. In other words, it is synonymous with liberty.
Under such a system, individuals would simply be left
free to do as they chose; compulsion would disappear;
the only bonds in society would be moral bonds." [23]

There could be no inherent objection to calling Jesus
this sort of anarchist if his teachings were sufficiently
distinct to justify the use of any political term. It
might, indeed, by its sensational connections attract
new attention to his words. It would not be the
first time novelty has done yeoman service as truth.
And it must be admitted that at first glance there is
something of similarity between Jesus' words and this
benign and harmless political metaphysics, which, like
a sheep in wolf's clothing, is doing its best by mas-
querading under an ill-omened name to startle the
world into believing it of practical importance. But
unless our conception of the teaching of Jesus is altogether incorrect, not only would it be ill-advised to
use the term anarchy in speaking of his teaching, but
it would commit him to notions of government and
society which were utterly absent from his thought.
For instance, much of the plausibility of this ironic
anarchy depends upon the conception of the state as
a mere coercive regulator of individuals who need an

[23] Salter, *Anarchy or Government*, 7. Two other opinions may
be requoted from this little work: "In heaven nothing like what we
call government on earth can exist" (Channing, *Works*, 361). "Strict
anarchy may be the highest conceivable grade of perfection of
social existence; but, if all men spontaneously did justice and loved
mercy, it is plain that all swords might advantageously be turned
into ploughshares, and that the occupation of judges and police
would be gone" (Huxley, *Essays*, I, 39).

umpire to decide and enforce the extent to which each must yield to the other in the interest of social peace. Once conceive of the state as something more than this agent of coercion, and the most captivating argument of the anarchist weakens before some utopia of the socialist pure and simple. Now the words of Jesus should not be forced to train with those of either school. He stands no more committed to an idea of government as a keeper of the peace than to the idea of government as a sort of executive committee of a democracy. In certain particulars his teaching would agree with either conception. But the point of its agreement is not within the sphere of speculative or practical politics, but within that of individual attitudes. One can no more call him an anarchist because he gives no political teaching than one can call him a surgeon because he never speaks of medicines.

Was then Jesus a socialist, a monarchist, a democrat? Again must it be said he was none of these. He was without political teaching. In this particular he is unique among the great teachers who have affected the West. Others, like Plato and Mahomet, have yielded to the temptation of systematic thought or circumstances, and have weighted their philosophy and their religion with political teachings that were either so ideal as to be impracticable or so practicable as to be outgrown. Jesus felt the force of the same temptation.[24] It was not through apathy that he refused to enter the sphere of political thought. He was teaching revolutionists. The people demanded political leadership, the professional teachers expected it, the Romans finally executed him for it. But with

[24] Matt. 4:8.

that concentration and foresight that continually grows upon the student of his life, he held himself sternly to the duties of a preacher of goodwill. It was enough when he had shown the fatherly monarchy of God and the supremacy of an all-embracing attitude.

If men desire the sanction of Jesus for any form of government, they must appeal not to specific sayings, but to his spirit. The test of a theory or a program must not be, does Jesus teach it? but does it make for fraternity?

IV

The bearing of the teaching of Jesus upon political affairs is thus the same as in the case of other social institutions. It contains no directions for social legislation. The supreme duty of man is to embody the principle of love in whatever social groupings he may be. As there must be not only the Christian home and the Christian organization of economic life, so the state must be regarded as a unit in which those who would embody the principle of Jesus are involved. This is only to repeat that the Christian cannot isolate himself from his social relations. A Christian father cannot act as if he were without a family; a Christian citizen cannot act as if there were no citizenship. The motives and attitudes which he derives from his experience as a Christian must be normative in his political life just as in all other social groupings.

Such general statements as these would probably not arouse difference of opinion. The real difficulty lies in determining just how to express the attitude of Jesus in political relations. There are those who would attempt to apply to the actions of political units his absolute idealism given to those possessed of no share in the government and who thought there was to be no history. Sometimes, as in the case of certain sects, this means that the Christian refuses to act as a civil magistrate, much less as a soldier.

Generally, however, this attempt to apply the absolute ideal of Jesus to human affairs without recognition of civic groupings takes the form of pacifism, with special emphasis upon the epigrams of Jesus that urge the turning of the cheek and nonresistance to evil. To such interpreters of Jesus war is murder. As a matter of interpretation this is certainly open to serious objection. There is no more justification in making one saying of Jesus the center of a Christion legalism than another. The same Jesus that said "turn the other cheek" also advised his disciples to sell their coats and buy swords.[25] The same Jesus who said "resist not evil" regarded himself as binding the strong man, and told his disciples to lend to everyone that asked. A saying of Jesus can be used safely only as it is interpreted as an epigrammatic emphasis of his fundamental position.

Beyond question war as an institution is opposed to the spirit of Jesus. But the attitude of goodwill does not determine the technique by which goodwill should be expressed. To seek to persuade a government to outlaw war and to substitute arbitration for war as a means of adjusting international disputes is clearly an application of the attitude of love to national affairs. In the same proportion as it succeeds will war disappear. There is no alternative goal for a Christianized politics.

But this is different from saying that the Christian

[25] Lk. 22:35-38.

citizen should not engage in a specific war. A man
cannot arbitrarily dissociate himself from his civic
relations. The nation itself has duties in which he
shares. There have been wars which were so obviously
the outcome of the attitudes that Jesus opposed as
to make it impossible for a Christian to support them.
But there have been and for a long time may be other
circumstances in which to engage in a war is a choice
between two evils. As over against war may be the
probable destruction of institutions which preserve an
approach toward the socializing of the Christian attitude. In such a case the question whether to share
in or to separate oneself from the national defense is
one which is not to be answered by turning a non-
political saying of Jesus into a political imperative.
There must be an intelligent balancing of possible
goods. The principle of neighborliness means the protection of victims of possible injustice just as truly
as caring for their sufferings after they have been
abused. Suppose that the Good Samaritan had arrived
in time to see the robbers maltreating their victim.
Would not his duty as a neighbor have involved his
interference by force with their robbery?

The organization of duties from the point of view
of social processes involves a group's or nation's relation to social history and progress. So far as one can
see in the words of Jesus there is no recognition of
process; but, as has been pointed out, the expression
of unconditioned ideals which human welfare demands
should be regnant in human affairs. But these ideals
are attitudes rather than programs. Just how they
are to be expressed may be a matter of opinion, but
it is unchristian to charge another person with being
unchristian who in an effort to attain ultimate human

good gives consideration to the obligations which social institutions like the state involve. War must be shown to involve losses of human progress greater than the losses resulting from non-resistance. But if these latter losses appear greater, and men refuse to protect their institutions, the principle of love is itself subordinated to a revived legalism justified by appeal to sayings of Jesus not intended to be political.[26]

V

But can a nation become a moral integer capable of expressing the attitude of goodwill? Certainly in history it has never been so regarded. Civil rights have been extended across frontiers only in accordance with definite treaties and agreements. Nations as such have always felt that there are certain matters which are not justiciable. In them the ultimate recourse is war.

The fundamental difficulty is that nations have not regarded themselves as belonging to a group related to them as society is to the individual. Sovereignty has been nonsocial and the development of international *mores* has therefore been slow. The attitudes of Jesus, however incorporated in individuals living in their social groupings, have not been seriously carried over into the relation of nations because of this fact. The very basis of a national morality has been wanting.

Yet the beginning of an international ethics can be seen. If, for example, one were to compare what Josephus calls the laws of war with those elements of present international law respected by nations at

[26] For a fuller discussion I may refer to my *Patriotism and Religion.*

war, it would be apparent that there has been moral progress. With Josephus the laws of war meant the right of the conqueror to treat the conquered as if they had no rights. To-day noncombatants are protected and there are limitations to many practices which two thousand years ago would have been regarded as conventional in war. Furthermore, because of the increase of rapid communication and the resulting contraction of our world, there has also grown the sense of mutual interest which a neighborhood always engenders. Arbitration has in many cases replaced the appeal to arms, and despite mutual suspicions nations are apparently growing ready to refer their differences to a world court or to pledge each other not to appeal to war as a means of settling disputes. There has grown up also on the part of certain nations the recognition of the rights of weaker nations.

If it be replied that self-interest operates in these advances, and that the reason why nations have grown less piratical is the increasing cost of piracy, the answer is that it makes very little difference what the causes are from which good morals emerge. When once a custom has been established one can forget its checkered pedigree. The significant thing is that it has been established.

But the idealism of no nation will rise above the spirit of its people. It is just here that there appears the significance of the Christian church as the institution pledged to the ideals and the attitudes of Jesus. Whatever its weaknesses and mistakes, organized Christianity has always held before the eyes of humanity the picture of one who sought to benefit others at the expense of his own life. As this attitude becomes socialized, it is not difficult to see it reappearing in various institutions of life. The last to be distinctly affected is the state, but even here the development of a sense of justice is traceable. It is to this development that we must look for the abolition of war. But war will not cease until these economic conditions from which it springs have themselves come under the censorship of the Christian attitude. It is as idle to think of stopping war while men are warlike and nations are acquisitive as it is to think of stopping pain while a man is diseased. The attitude of nations as well as of individuals must be purged of acquisitiveness and brutality, and their relations with one another must come under the general law of love, that is to say, of group relations which make possible coöperative action.

It is not enough to say that if a nation is composed of good people it will act wisely or altruistically. Even if all of its citizens were thoroughly Christian—a condition which is certainly contrary to fact—there would still be the problem of the corporate action of the entire nation. While the moral attitude and ideals of individuals must be high if a nation is to be genuinely moral, there still remains the task of Christianizing the attitude of governments. Politics, both national and international, must some day express the attitude of Jesus if civilization is to be a blessing. Just as in economic life, before a group morality developed, a man could be a good friend in noneconomic relations while a remorseless competitor in the field of business, so the people of a state may be kindly and philanthropic outside the field of politics and at the same time warlike wherever national interests are affected. It is only as those higher attitudes which possess indi-

viduals are socialized and applied to relations in the
large group of nations that the influence of Jesus will
be felt in the institutions of a state. Expert knowledge of statecraft is necessary for the expression of
such new national ideals. Good intentions are no
absolute guaranty of the worth of policy. We need
intelligent statesmanship for the technique of national
relations just as truly as we need the nationalized
Christian attitude to determine its policies. Among
the first steps toward the accomplishment of such a
rational and desirable end is to see to it that international policies are set by departments of state
rather than by those of war and navy. It can hardly
be expected that professional interest in war should
be an incentive to set up conditions which will end
war.

If one is to treat Jesus seriously, practical considerations should not distract attention from the heart of
his message. That upon which Jesus relied as the
divinely ordered social force is not sagacity but goodwill. If the world's experience counts for anything,
no war can be fought except by cultivating hatred.
However much our passions may be clothed in idealistic language, and however tragically necessary it
may become, war at best can be justified only as
a choice between two evils, and not between a good
and an evil. The will to conquer means that a nation
must abandon kindliness toward its enemy. Soldiers
cannot be taught to love their enemies; their business
is to kill them. Nations that go to war must abandon
for the time being attempts at doing each other justice; they must crush one another. And the psychology of hatred does not end with victory. It lives on,
diverted from national enemies to any person or insti-

tution interfering with our individual or our class prejudices. Loyalty to one's nation, readiness to go to war to protect the institutions which are the agencies of human sympathy and to prevent the destruction of the accomplishments of democracy and developing personal rights—these may sometimes be legitimate. But they are at best an unhappy adjustment of method to a purpose. To hate, to kill, to injure others, are not within the ideals of Jesus. A nationalism that relies upon such means to accomplish national power is not his.

VIII.

JESUS AND THE CHURCH

JESUS spoke even less about the church than about the state. The reason is plain—there was no church for him to discuss. Government, wealth, family, social customs were in his world, but that vast organization which bears his name had not yet been born. He did not contemplate founding a new religion and his immediate followers never detached themselves from their national faith. Jesus recognized the sanitary requirements of the Mosaic law,[1] the custom of offering sacrifices.[2] He took part in the services of the synagogue and attempted to reform the administration of the Temple area. He opposed religious teachers because they were making the law of no avail through their tradition.[3] He established a group within Judaism, which with difficulty came later to see that it could admit others than Jews. Only when, outside of Palestine, groups were formed of those who were not Jews did the movement which he had founded take on the aspect of a separate religion. There are only two of the sayings attributed to Jesus in which the word *ecclesia,* which came subsequently to mean organized Christianity, is used,[4] and in both cases the translation "group" or "community" is preferable to

[1] Mk. 1:40-45; Lk. 17:11-19.   [3] Mk. 7:13; Matt. 15:6.
[2] Matt. 5:23, 24.   [4] Matt. 16:18; 18:17.

121

"church." This group is the parent of the later church, but it is historically incorrect to read back into the little company of revolutionists to whom he was teaching goodwill the structure, the rites, the creeds, the priesthood, or the theology of later centuries. Within this group Jesus would have no social cleavage which orders involve. The kings of the Gentiles might have lordship over their subjects and those that exercised authority might be called benefactors, but it was not to be so with the Twelve, though they were to sit on thrones judging the twelve tribes of Israel.[5] Those who wished to become first were to be the servants of all. They were all brothers.[6]

Certainly in its earliest forms the Christian movement was nontheological, nonecclesiastical, without priest or preacher, a group of people who believed that Jesus as the Christ was coming back to restore the kingdom of Israel and give them the joys which they already began to portray.[*] They were generous, enthusiastic, prayerful, and attentive to the teaching of the apostles. They did not break with the Temple or the synagogue. When, later, many little groups of believers sprang up over the Roman Empire, the fact that they were not composed of Jews exclusively or at all naturally led to a need of rites and organization. But as the institution developed, the character of the Christians remained obvious to all. "Behold how these Christians love one another," was the comment of the non-Christian observer. The Christians regarded themselves, in fact, as constituting a third race, and they devoted themselves to acts of philanthropy. In the ancient world the social motivation that lies in love, and the pressure for organization which social

[5] Lk. 22:25-30; Mk. 10:42-44.   [6] Matt. 23:8.

needs develop, were prevented from finding expression in society and the economic life, and naturally turned inward to the life of the Christian society itself. In consequence, when the Roman Empire collapsed the church found itself prepared to take up many of the social obligations which the Empire had abandoned. The pressure of circumstances, the violence of opposition, the growing identification of ecclesiastical with technique, and such technique is a matter of science* political interests, all tended to develop an institution which was not foreseen by Jesus himself.

But, as has already appeared, the group was essential to the plans of Jesus. Though the kingdom did not come as it expected, the group was the depository of his teaching, the conserver of the spiritual heritage of his influence. And so it came about that, although we have no teaching of Jesus concerning the church, we have a vast amount of teaching by the church about Jesus.

I

Sooner or later goodwill becomes a problem of social rather than of motive. Roughly speaking, society breaks into two classes: those who wish to exploit their fellows and those who wish to coöperate with them for the common good. It is true that these two motives often alternate in an individual's life, but the one or the other becomes dominant whenever the interests of the individual are set up as rivals to those of the group to which he belongs. But how are those who really have goodwill to apply it? They cannot safely trust their prejudices and impulses. Of the various courses of action proposed, goodwill implies that the most effectively helpful be selected. The father's love for his sick child is not intelligent until he uses the best remedies. So in the case of those who wish to reproduce the attitude of Jesus. Goodwill is a social leaven which must give rise to organized customs and procedure. In a world growing ever more complicated, the organization of groups each having its particular function is the method by which humanity satisfies its multiplying needs. Social order is impossible without the state; sex-morality demands the family; economic life has its corporations and labor unions; education has its schools and universities; the religion of Jesus has the church.

Honesty compels the student of the teaching of Jesus to admit that as legislative directions for social life it is as yet impracticable. Society as we know it cannot be without divorce, a state cannot rest upon either passive acceptance or political indifference, economic life cannot exist on universal charity. Neither history nor rational hope for the future can see in to-day's humanity a body of men and women unanimously and sacrificially devoted to personal ends. Christians may hope that the kingdoms of this world may become the kingdoms of their God and of his Christ, but if they have any real understanding of human nature they have no right to expect that every man and woman will be swayed by the ideals of Jesus. This may be a lamentable fact, but any realistic estimate of the significance of Jesus in our world must not yield to myopic optimism. Jesus himself had no illusions as to human nature. He said frankly that the easy way and the broad gate were preferred by the multitude to the narrow way and the strait gate.[7] No wealth of pious vocabulary can change the situa-

[7] Matt. 7:13, 14.

tion. Those who choose to see the world that should be in the world that is will find themselves gloomy spectators rather than participants in social progress. A Mishna, composed of the sayings of Jesus, would be far less practicable than the Mishna derived by the rabbis from the law of Moses. For while Moses was a statesman dealing with actual human conditions, Jesus was a champion of an absolute timeless ideal which he said would be put into operation only by those who dared to be martyrs. But if martyrdom became universal, how could social justice progress?

The difficulty in treating Jesus' sayings as social legislation has always been admitted. This will account for the inconsistencies on the part of those who choose this or that text as the center of a social system. Those who made celibacy and poverty indispensable for the imitation of their Master withdrew from the world, yet were forced to form economic groups in monasteries and convents. But they never expected that all humanity would become celibate or beggars. Saints needed sinners to continue the race and furnish means of support. Those who make Jesus' sayings regarding nonresistance central have not undertaken either to be celibate or to give to all who ask alms. Men who wish to make Jesus into a social legislator invariably choose the particular saying they seek to obey. The grounds for their choice they do not state, for the man who undertakes to live by the law, whether it be that of Moses or Jesus or the United States of America, can have no higher law without abandoning his own position.

But if Jesus' teaching is not legislation, what is it? Exactly what it purports to be—teaching intended to evoke an attitude of soul. Jesus was no more a social legislator because he talked about human hopes, religious trust, and absolute ideals toward which men should move than William Cullen Bryant was an ornithologist because he wrote about a waterfowl, or Browning a music master because he wrote on Abt Vogler. The real social influence of Jesus to-day does not lie in his words but in men and women who endeavor to express in social relations and institutions the attitudes which he himself taught and embodied.

Thus there must be within the group of groups we call Society one composed of persons who, with the enthusiasm of the revolutionists Jesus gathered about himself, will commit themselves to the adventure of reproducing in their lives, in their social relations and in all groups of which they are members the attitude of Jesus. Such a decision does not presuppose a technical knowledge of economics or politics or any other science of human action. Those who compose such a group may be unlearned as well as scholars, poor as well as prosperous, married as well as single, little known as well as statesmen. Except in rare instances, they cannot separate themselves from social groups in which the complications of life have placed them. If they are wise they will not undertake to live as if society is what some day they hope it may become. They will not permit their faith in God to hypnotize them into forgetting that some of those before whom they are tempted to cast their pearls are swine, or that whoever would be as harmless as a dove needs to be as wise as a serpent. Much less will they think that love of itself will always show the way to safe conduct, or that good intentions guarantee good sense.

But despite all limitations which practical wisdom will set upon their hopes and conduct, they will none the less be committed to following Jesus. And as such followers, they can see clearly that if his and their attitude could be socialized the problem of human welfare would not be answered by acquisitiveness and coercion, but by goodwill.

II

The church as an institution evolved from the group of revolutionists Jesus gathered to found a community of brothers. It must perpetuate and socialize that community's spirit.

However changed the Christian movement may have become as it has appropriated the customs of different epochs and ideas of other religions, it is none the less true that its central principle is that of loyalty to the ideals of its founder. The fact that he refused to adjust his teachings to the civilization of his own day makes it all the more necessary for his modern followers to make the adjustment to our present situation. The real test of the vitality of a movement is precisely at the point where it attempts to adjust the ideals of the past to conditions in the present. *

The church as an institution has never been indifferent to social affairs, but historically viewed, its primary purpose has been to mediate salvation from hell by pleading the merits of Christ before an angry God. The death of Christ has been less utilized as an incentive to sacrificial social-mindedness than as an agency by which the mercy of God can be gained. Indirectly it has been a constant suggestion to service and sacrifice. Directly, however, it has too often been an agency of acquisitiveness—the getting of salvation. All efforts to stimulate organized Christianity to a

larger emphasis upon the social attitude of Jesus have
been opposed by those to whom such a policy would
have been expensive. Men have been ready to send
missionaries to preach to non-Christian people a message of salvation from hell, but have not been ready
to protect the same people from the curse of trade in
narcotics or to check their governments in the seizure
of land and the deposition of native governments.
This is not to say that the church should be indifferent
to the *post mortem* welfare of mankind, but it is to
say that as an institution the Christian church has
generally been slow to champion changes that in any
way affected the economic or the political *status quo*.

In a measure this hesitation is warranted. It is a
dangerous thing to interfere with a going social order.
In reform we need something more than a desire to
remedy injustice. Only recall the effects of the undis-
ciplined generosity of the French nobility on August 4,
1789. It is hard for most people to realize that economic and political adjustments require as expert
social technicians as do medicine or surgery. A man
who would not think of permitting his neighbor to
prescribe for a sick child will unhesitatingly adopt
that neighbor's theory as to money or the organization
of government. The church certainly cannot afford
to commit itself to any program that will not bear
scientific investigation.

As one group among many it has its primary function. If it is really loyal to Jesus it must stand for
his conception that love is basic and that regardless
of all social and cultural injustice men are free to make
love effective. It must stimulate the sense of the
divine presence and bring men into a realization of
fellowship with the divine. But it cannot stop with

ritual or doctrine. It must evoke in men and women the same moral attitudes as those which Jesus himself embodied. It must convince the world not only of sin and righteousness and judgment, but also that love is a practicable basis for social relations.

It cannot, however, perform such a function if it deals only with abstractions. It must itself be a sort of trial laboratory in which its own teachings are tested in its social organization, and it must act collectively where collective action is demanded in a moral crisis.

It is to the credit of the church that, despite the tremendous pressure of brutality and ignorance with which mankind is handicapped, it has accomplished so much in these directions, but to a very considerable extent these accomplishments have been due to the trial and error method. We are too intelligent at the present time to adopt anything so costly. If love is sincere it will not be content until it has found the best and most efficient means of rendering service to others. The world is at the present time too intelligent to undertake in the name of religion to make any single saying of Jesus self-operative. If his attitude is to be expressed in social institutions, it can only be after intelligent investigation and scientific advice. Hospitals and medical training are just as truly the expression of his spirit as was washing one's face in the pool of Siloam. So in government. A vote may be as much an expression of the Christian attitude as an unwillingness to lead revolt against a conqueror. A just levy of taxes, a recognition of human values in industry may be just as much the expression of his will as the giving of alms. Neither a man nor a community can afford to let goodwill exclude scientific ability in the choice of programs and techniques for group activity.

In the last analysis social progress is not a matter of systems but of folks. And folks can be made brotherly in heart and coöperative in action by an institution having such a function. For methods of action they and it can call upon the social sciences.

III

One aspect of the institutional technique of the Christian church is what is commonly known as social service. In this it is already being given scientific assistance. Alongside of the Christian ministry have grown up vocations which, far beyond the limits of church programs, deal with human welfare, charity, public recreation, and similar interests. The ministry no longer is the only calling in which the idealism of youth can find self-expression. Men and women possessed of vicarious interest in human welfare are more numerous to-day than ever before, but they find a wide range of opportunity for self-expression. The church can now see in other agencies of human welfare fellow members of the vicarious tenth of society. Indeed, it suffers somewhat in the new competition, because men and women can serve their fellows through social agencies without committing themselves to theological tenets.

The fact that so large a proportion of those adopting the new social vocations come from the sphere of the church's influence argues that Christianity is again finding new institutional expression. Nor is this anything revolutionary. The past four hundred years show a steady progress away from strictly ecclesiastical modes of expressing Christian attitudes. The Protestant state churches, the Nonconformist Protestants, the Free Churches which developed in the eighteenth century, the Young Men's and Young Women's Christian Associations, all mark stages in the process. The present organization of social service which so clearly represents the ethical ideals of Jesus is the contribution of the twentieth century to institutional Christianity.

The present development of social agencies accordingly makes it unnecessary for the churches to carry on many community operations which formerly they alone were fitted to direct. Trained and specialized leadership can do these things much better than amateur altruists.

But such a delegation of duty to the new agencies does not imply that the churches lack opportunities for equally intelligent social service. In them are activities and institutions which the community is not ready to establish, but which later it may take over. In the field of initial experiment the churches are not rivals or even competitors of other social agencies. They represent all the organized altruism many a community possesses. Without them such altruism would be either dormant or without channels of expression. Cases in which social agencies are established in a community where there is no church are few. That institutions started by the church should pass into more specialized hands is to be expected, and, generally speaking, hastened. But a community must have groups of altruistic citizens before it can have its own altruistic institutions. Men cannot gather social figs from individual thistles.

Thus the relationship between social agencies and the church is reciprocal. Just as the church can fur-

nish men and women of goodwill and keep the fires of
altruism burning by religious conviction, social agencies can serve the church even beyond acting as its
agents. Indeed, they are already giving the church
a conception of the content and the limitations of
moral judgments. Our new knowledge of the blight
resting upon ill-born, ill-nourished, and physically
unfit children is certain to modify or make intelligible
the church's conception of sin. The more we know
about pedigrees, the better we understand morality.
Good lunches and good teeth make for good temper.
Case study in mental hygiene, housing, the rescue of
children from bad surroundings, and similar activities
are all uniting to induce a conception of morality
which is far less concerned with the Garden of Eden
than with the town and the environment in which one
lives. The prevention of tuberculosis and syphilis is
quite as much an element of duty as the maintenance
of church-going. Our growing understanding of actual
human life is making it plain that the church cannot
reduce sin and righteousness, forgiveness and regeneration to a theological algebra. New moral ideals and
new reconstructive methods are actually evolving from
that estimate of individuals and society given by social
science.

IV

The growth of social interest outside the church,
however, emphasizes anew the fact that the church is
to have a fundamentally religious function. True, a
few radicals seem to hold that social and cutural activity is the primary, if not the only, function of a church.
They would substitute sociology and psychology for
theology, and social activities, moving-pictures, basket-

ball games, political discussions, for the conventional activities of the church. Such a view deprives religion of any other than social validity and makes the church one social institution among many.

Just as a few years ago we were told that eugenics was to accomplish more than the Ten Commandments, so now we are encouraged to believe that society will find some new technique for the church which will enable it to escape the evils of so-called supernaturalism. This technique seems to be found pretty largely in the field of medicine and surgery, sanitation, amusement, and recreation. In this pursuit of morals without God, and utopias without repentance, the churches are asked to join. It is of course conceded that they will at least for the present preserve vestigial religious organs, such as the choir, prayer-like meditation, an address, and a collection. But religion itself is to be a sociology and an ethic.

If this conception of the function of the Christian church is correct, religion is psychopathic. The sooner such churches are replaced by frankly and consistently non-religious social agencies, the better. A church as a church loses its grip on humanity about in the same proportion as it fails to stand for something which is religious in the sense of a relation between man and that immanent reason, purpose, and love upon which he is dependent and from which he seeks to draw help.* For this, if for no other reason, the church can be counted on to develop and advance a sound basis for the correct social attitude. It grounds its advocacy of justice and goodwill in God's love. Whether or not individuals may be religious, no one can be so blind as to fail to see that this conception is tremendously dynamic. Furthermore, it is preservative of enthusiasm. Cynicism always besets those who are themselves devoted to the amelioration of human sin and stupidity. The church, if not the only, is certainly the chief agency for lifting social duty with its self-sacrifice from professional routine into human brotherhood. It is more blessed to give than to receive only when one feels the urge of love like that of Jesus.

The church is a social institution in which group life is being educated in goodwill. But such a process needs something more than an institution content with social amelioration. The true descendants of the original group about Jesus will be those who possess something of the revolutionary attitude. Not that they will wish to destroy violently existing institutions, but they will be adventurous, unwilling to progress by looking backward. The institutions of religion are always in danger of becoming stereotyped, ministering to the *status quo*. The Christian church must inspire and educate men to sacrifice social status or economic privilege in the interests of others less happily situated. True, great vested interests, whether ecclesiastical or commercial, seldom surrender their advantages without struggle. The very success of the Christian movement has naturally gathered within itself, as Jesus foresaw, many who are not his true followers.[8] Too often the church as an organization has been on the defensive, holding its gates against the assault of evil rather than charging victoriously against the gates of hell.

But there has always been a leaven of sacrificial idealism within the mass of ecclesiastical organization.

[8] Matt. 14:47-50. Cf. also the "little apocalypse" of Matt. 25:31-46.

There have always been men who undertook to take Jesus seriously and whose faith was contagious and pervasive. It is they rather than the great mass of professional representatives of Jesus who really signify. They are the city set on the hill; they are the lamp not placed under a bushel. To such persons the endeavor to reproduce the attitude of Jesus is not a drab duty but an inspiring opportunity. They really believe that love can be in some way institutionalized, and that the group as well as the individuals can express the spirit of Jesus.

And why should they be mistaken? Is it not of the very genius of humanity to accomplish by group action what could never be within the power of individuals, no matter how numerous? Human history does not tend toward mobs, but toward institutions. If the attitude of love is to express itself it cannot overlook this law of life. Coöperative action must express the same sort of ideals as that of the individual. Human life cannot dissociate itself from institutions seeking to perpetuate the best experience and to make human conditions more personal. Nor can it fail to see the danger which lies in coöperative action and institutions of the opposite sort.

It is therefore a matter of course that there should be men and women down through the ages who, seeing the discrepancy between social policies and the ideal which Jesus committed to his community, have sought to make the church an agent of social transformation. Nor are they lacking to-day. Despite the blight of hatred and misunderstanding, of selfishness and sensuality, which has fallen upon so much of our world, the institutionalizing of the spirit of Jesus is not neglected. Not only are individuals seeking to reproduce the attitude of Jesus, but they are expressing his attitude in their coöperative activities.

No man whose historical knowledge and ability is more than that of a vocabulary can fail to see the significance of the church as an institution in preserving and developing social ideals, social organization, and social rebirth. When one stops to consider the extraordinary cataclysms across which Christianity has carried humanity during the past two thousand years, its social capacity is amazing. Think only of the crisis which arose when a great and brilliant civilization disintegrated, cities disappeared, literature was destroyed, works of art were buried, political institutions were abandoned, citizens were massacred, and hordes of armed immigrants inherited a land they had conquered! Yet that was the crisis in civilization which the church had to face in the fourth and fifth centuries. The Dark Ages and the brutality of the Middle Ages are not chargeable to the church. They were the result of social forces which the church had to withstand and transform. And despite all difficulties, it did its work. The only learning was in its circles, the only social ideals were in its teaching, the only social service was in its institutions. But hardly had it made possible the wonderful thirteenth century, when the discovery of America and other causes brought about a complete dislocation of economic, political, and educational life. Again the church had to face a crisis such as no other religion has been able to face. Again the church survived and gave direction to the Renaissance and Revolutionary periods of the sixteenth century. So, too, when in the eighteenth century the stress of the new industrial life in

Europe and America brought the middle class to power. This period of revolution was not merely political; it was still another shifting of the entire perspective of life. At the start it seemed as if Christianity was to give way to some sort of illumination, or philosophy, or proletarian impracticability; but great religious movements like those of the Methodists, Baptists, and Evangelicals of the Church of England produced men, cultivated attitudes of mind, and organized social agencies which lie at the bottom of the social welfare program of modern times.

But in all this activity the church has not relied merely on social technique. It has had power to minister to social needs because it has stood for the cosmic reason working in evolution, for God in human life, for dynamic morals rather than social conventions, and above all, because it sought, with such intelligence as culture permitted, to institutionalize the attitude of Jesus. Relieved from the pressure of innumerable social duties, the church can more effectively devote itself to its own task of producing men and women of faith and goodwill and of training them in the art of coöperative living in a real world. It can thus become the manual-training school of social life rather than the exclusive agent of social service.

Nor is this all. Back of every institutional activity there lies some spiritual force without which the institutions themselves would decline. Persons devoted to the details of administration put on the protective covering of unsentimental impersonality. It is fortunate that this is the case. No social worker could endure prolonged contact with misery, sorrow, and want without this instinctive method of protection. But humanity is more than its instincts and its bodies.

Behaviorism is only a half-truth. We believe in justice and kindliness and the worth of our fellow men. Any institution which can produce people of goodwill is indispensable if society is to grow better. The community of those seeking to embody the attitudes of Jesus is this sort of institution *par excellence*. Possessed now of trustworthy means for expressing goodwill in society, it can safely stimulate sympathy and sacrificial social-mindedness.

Goodwill itself demands a basis. Why should the strong organize to care for the weak, or the fortunate to care for the unfortunate, unless there be some fundamental reason for this violation of the law of the survival of the physically fittest to survive? In humanity there must be something even more fit than strength, else our care for the weak and for the diseased, the depressed and the dependent, may be only a weakening of the race itself. Regard for human welfare implies that human welfare is worth preserving.

An institution which seeks to make men more brotherly by inculcating the ethical message of Jesus and his faith in the God of love will furnish the material for a new society. Agencies for rendering social service will organize this material and train it for service. Both alike heartily coöperating in the pursuit of fraternity can lead men not only to ameliorate human ills but to set up social practices which shall evolve more normal, more permanent, and more equitable relations between men. Upon such coöperation our confidence in a better social order can hopefully rest. For the recognition that social service is a means rather than a goal will accustom our world to that attitude of mind and that social behavior which

individuals and classes and nations must possess if
ever that glad day is to dawn when mankind realizes
that it is more blessed to give justice than to fight for
rights.

V

If the church is really to institutionalize the spirit
and the attitude of Jesus it must be more than one of
many agencies of scientific social technique. By its
origin and history it stands committed to a faith in
God as love. Only thus can it be said to have the mind
of Christ. And only as it makes such faith contagious
and controlling is it following in his way.

The difficulty in such a belief is evident enough, for
it involves one's attitude toward concrete life. If God
is good, can he be really all-powerful? If he were,
would he permit men to suffer? If he were both good
and powerful, how can one explain the crimes and
merciless brutality of men who thought they were
doing him service? The thinkers of the church have
always recognized these difficulties. Conceiving God
as an absolute sovereign, it was incredible to them that
he should not punish the ways that in their opinion
had become rebellious. That he had shown his love
was evident, they believed, but there lingered within
their minds the suspicion that in some way his
sovereignty might have been impaired. To meet this
difficulty they turned to Jesus, and in the field of transcendentalized politics magnified his spirit of love. It
was he, because he loved the world, that bore the sins
of the world.

That such a theology did not always produce the
attitude of Jesus in the minds of his followers was due
partly to the fact that they still thought of God as an

absolute sovereign, and partly to their prescientific ignorance of group morality. To no small degree the same difficulty persists to-day in the minds of many persons. They are ready to have Jesus pay the debt they owe to God, but they do not see that a similar attitude toward all aspects of life is involved in their loyalty to him. Much less do they realize that faith in God as Father involves something of tremendous significance to all social relations. Theology here has not adequately represented Jesus. He was not concerned to prove that the Father was unbegotten. To him God was no metaphysical problem, but one to be trusted in serene confidence that his will was good. For this the church ought to stand, not only in the case of individuals, but in the case of group action. To express this attitude in social activity is something more than to relieve the unfortunate. It is to remove the causes that produce human suffering. It is not enough to play the Good Samaritan on the road from some Jerusalem to some Jericho—the road itself should be policed. It is not enough to save brands from the burning—we must put out the fire.

As one among many social institutions the church cannot be indifferent to the fact that if an individual is to be personal he must act from within some group. Even in his conflict with group attitudes he must find others with whom he can coöperate. The history of humanity is not written in terms of individuals or of society, but in individuals in society. Any religious organization that disregards the ethical nature of group action is attempting to set up a reform against nature.

Yet caution is here imperative. In our partially democratized world individuals can carry into one group the attitudes which have been evoked and cul-

tivated in another. In fact, one of the chief characteristics of democracy is the membership in groups
with different functions. The multiplicity of such
relationships is quite as important as the freedom of
membership in any single group. In democracy,
theoretically at least, the boundary of interest of one
group is not to be the same as that of other groups.
Freedom and equality are threatened when membership in one group is made the condition of membership
in another. It is this danger that the church constantly faces. On the one hand a religious organization may try to control other institutions and insist
that political or other preferences must be determined
by religious relations. This would lead to precisely the
sort of thing against which Jesus warned his disciples,
that is, the use of coercion for furthering good ends.
The passions engendered by religion are as strong as
those aroused by sex or desire for property. When by
any chance they become identified with other social
interests, violence and suffering become unendurable.
There is no more terrible person than the man who
believes that it is the will of his God that he make
other people suffer because of religious error.

It is therefore with great hesitation that the church
should undertake to act in other than religious and
moral fields. Its main object is to utilize the group
spirit for the purpose of religious experience, to establish an institution in which there may be moral instruction in the ideals and attitudes of Jesus, and one which
at the same time can give a sort of manual training in
the principles it is inculcating.

And yet, as a group within other groups, it has the
obligation not simply to train individuals in attitudes
which can be expressed in their social relations, but

also to act as a group having relation with other groups. The past few years have seen very considerable expression of a public opinion of the different church organizations on social matters. The sublime faith in the love of God which the Christian community inherits from its founder constitutes the social gospel. Too often men have forgotten this confidence in listening to the call of duty. Unless the church stands for this it will lose its vitality and significance. Its social message is not primarily to the unprivileged to acquire privilege, but to those who have privilege to trust in the practicability of love and to share with those with less privilege. Safety and comfort may lie in other directions. It is easier to promise heaven to dissatisfied wage earners than to raise their wages. It is easier to transfer denominational enthusiasm to nonchristian lands than to rectify the conditions of life among coal-miners and steel-workers. It is easier to repeat the Apostles' Creed than to help bear the cross of the Master of the Apostles. If the church as an institution is to be loyal to Jesus it must not let ignorance set bounds to this loyalty. It must transform social forces.

It is therefore only what might have been expected that, over against the inherited view of the function of the churches, we should find a rapidly growing appreciation of their social obligations. The development of social work has reacted upon them, and to a considerable degree churches have begun to represent new social interests. The conception of religious education has materially broadened. It is no longer a mere teaching of the Bible, the catechism, and the "lesson helps," but a seeking to develop moral attitudes within all the spheres of life. If the nineteenth-century church discovered the needs of childhood, the twentieth century has discovered the needs of children. Kindergartens, nurseries, parents' classes, are growing common. Many churches have a complete outfit for community centers with the necessary apparatus for athletics, sociability, dramatics, and, of course, for dining; for if the kingdom of God is not eating and drinking, the modern church has learned to line the road to it with opportunities for the saints to refresh themselves. Quite as striking is the widespread avowal of loyalty to the Christ-spirit in wider social and economic fields. Denomination after denomination has adopted or enlarged the social creed drawn up by the Federal Council of the Churches of Christ in America. Although reactionaries may protest, and the elder statesmen of Christendom may warn, the generation now coming on to the stage of church life is full of social spirit.

When men first began to see this it was natural that they should trust too much to social organization and think it easier to convert humanity *en masse* than to induce individuals to accept whole-heartedly the ideals of Jesus. Sociology seemed an easier route than the way of religious experience. When it ended in the wilderness of human obstinacy, it was natural for men who had supposed social Christianity to be a substitute for personal religious living to grow uneasy. The kingdom of God they expected did not immediately appear. Only thus can one explain the present reactionary attitude of many preachers. But even they cannot reproduce the attitude of half a century ago. They are right in insisting that God must work in individual hearts and that there is no mechanical way in which to produce virtue. Those who really understood Jesus have always urged such religious individualism. We shall not lose our present apprehension of the social bearing of faith in God. We can no more revert to an atavistic individualism in religion than in business. The church has not been moving in circles but in spirals. If it looks out upon the worth of the individual with renewed interest in a mystical expression of the experience of religion, it sees this truth from a new elevation. The motives and the faith of Jesus we have come to see are not limited to individual men and women, but are equally applicable to the action of groups. For them, too, the church has a message of hope born of its faith in God and the consequent practicability of goodwill. An ideal incapable of dominating group action will inevitably lose its power with individuals.

Such a social gospel does not carry with it a program of economic or political activity. The church is not an economic or political institution. Administrative policies in these fields must be set up by men who not only have goodwill, but have also expert knowledge and experience. But none the less it does promise success to group altruism. In an issue among classes and nations which demands choice between a policy that is selfish and one less selfish, between one that seeks to give justice and one which seeks to maintain a privilege, the church as the institutional exponent of the principles of Jesus cannot safely hesitate. It cannot be silent when silence means consent to injustice or cowardice. There is no moral doubt as to the wrong in relying upon war as a method of settling international disputes, or as to the need of regulating the labor of women and children and the length of the working day, or as to the right of labor to collective bargaining. Why should not organized Christianity

champion—as it has—the better way? The position
of organized Christianity here is the same as in its use
of science. Religion did not give men the belief in
the flat earth or the round earth. That was given by
those who were regarded as having scientific authority.
Similarly as regards the organization of social processes.
In the one case as in the other, the church as the representative of fraternity must stand committed to that
in group action which is nearer to wisdom. Radicals
and all others incapable of seeing that men must act as
members of groups and that social transformation is a
process may grow impatient with the inability of men
to apply absolutely the sayings of Jesus to a modern
world. The probability is that the church is too
cautious in some of its social sympathies, but that it
has an institutional duty of bringing the conviction as
to the goodwill of God to other groups is certain. And
on all sides one can see the response to this conception.
However much those out of sympathy with the church
may publish its shortcomings, the fact remains that
within the church there are those who increasingly see
that the attitude of Jesus must be and can be embodied
in the attitude and official votes of that body of men
who stand committed to the belief that God's will is a
good will and that preparation for enjoying the blessings of goodwill consists in acting in accordance with it
both individually and collectively. Here again practical experience is showing that attitudes are more
than epigrams and that the reproduction of the attitude of Jesus is not independent of group action and
the laws of social evolution.*

IX.

THE SOCIAL GOSPEL OF JESUS

Does the result of our study of the social teaching of Jesus seem vague rather than practical? We have been told so many times that we are to go to him for directions in our social life that it may be disappointing to find him so lacking in specific counsel. Yet lacking in such counsel he is. Our age is industrial; his was agricultural and commercial. To-day women have the rights of persons; in his day they were under the control of father or husband. We enjoy—and endure—democracy, the sovereignty of the people; in the days of Jesus such a political conception was not even dreamed. We are aware of social processes and inquisitive as to the influences operative in human life; Jesus believed that history was to end and a new era begin by the interposition of God. Such contrasts make specific directions impracticable. Had Jesus told the people of his day how to live he would have told the people of this day how not to live. He never showed more wisdom than in his silence.

It may have been some instinctive recognition of these incongruities that has kept the Church movement from attempting to organize social customs and social practices by a literal application of the teaching of Jesus. His words have been judged too poetical for such application. Christian teachers and thinkers have set forth the significance of Jesus himself rather than

146

his specific teachings. So far has it been from being a mistake for Christianity to make the personality of Jesus superior to his isolated sayings that an attempt to do the opposite would repeatedly have checked progress toward larger personal freedom. The entire experience of the Christian centuries points to the necessity of the use of Jesus as something more than a teacher. Every age, like his first disciples, must view him as one who contributed to human society a life and an attitude rather than a philosophy and a system.

Jesus has had more than a casual influence on civilization. Whatever be one's theology, however far removed one may be from sympathy with the Christian church, the influence of Jesus is unescapable. History with him is not the same as history without him. When all allowance has been made for human frailties among Christians and generous justice has been rendered to other religions, still the sensational fact remains that modern civilization originated and developed among his followers in Western Europe and America. Imperfect though they are, the social institutions which are now transforming all human life bear the impress of his personality. To ignore Jesus is to ignore history. The very social atmosphere is charged with the memory of his sacrifice. The more men distrust formal Christianity the larger bulk the figure of its Founder and the group which he founded as the conservator of his teachings and spirit.

Such facts make it imperative to treat Jesus seriously. Men have always turned to him when guidance and courage were needed. In days when citizens were excluded from politics and social reform, they found him in metaphysics. When the Heavenly Father was all but obscured by the brutality of medieval society they found in him the crucified and atoning Savior. He has been the companion of the martyr, the *sans culotte* of the French revolutionist, the brother of the democrat. In our own day, men who feel themselves all but lost in the labyrinth of our social order look to him for guidance. But the one whom they seek is not the documentary problem of criticism, the synthetic myth of archæology, the personalized covenant of dogmatic theology, the gentlemanly martyr of romantic liberalism. The one real Jesus is the Jesus *of* history and the Jesus *in* history. And he is more than the Jesus of the gospels.

Two thousand years afford opportunity for once commanding figures to disappear into the mists of history and archeology. Few of the great men of the days of Jesus are now more than names symbolizing certain qualities. Even in our schools and colleges epochmakers like Julius Caesar, Augustus, and Marcus Aurelius seem hardly more than wraiths temporarily materialized in class examinations. But the characters which have enriched human lives with the gift of discipline or religious hope still sway human life. Gotama, Confucius, Mahomet—these still live in their followers. But compared with these historic persons Jesus is unique. He has become more than a long since dead individual who left words which are to be remembered and an organization which exists apart from him. His teachings have influence to-day as truly as those of Confucius, his inner experience is even more sanely individual than that of Gotama, he founded a great movement like Mahomet. Yet he is different from them all. His personality is more potent, his life is more exemplary, and his death is the center of the ritual and theology of a civilization that is transforming humanity. He has been built into history as an influence rather than a biography.

The age Jesus taught has long since passed, but his attitude is still a social heritage of direction and inspiration. To make this heritage available for a world so different from that in which Jesus himself lived is a matter of correct method and sacrificial social-mindedness. If the test of loyalty to him be the literal following of specific sayings in the gospels the whole Christian world would write itself down as hypocritical. But Jesus has done more than any lawgiver could do. He has contributed not only to the ideals but to the very dynamic of social life. His real influence is not dependent upon historical circumstances, Jewish civilization, or messianic expectations as to the future. As we have already seen, it is born of his own conception of his life experience as an interpretation of the true character of God, and it has grown as he has grown.

This social significance of Jesus involves three fundamental principles implicit in his ideal and attitude. In them is his social gospel.

I

Human life is not under the sole control of economic forces. Economic determinism or any other type of mechanistic philosophy is impossible for one who, like Jesus, believes in the loving care of God. There is no small need of this emphasis in our day. It is altogether too easy to draw our analogies of human life from the physicist's laboratory and the machine shop. Even when men turn psychologists they often seem to be more interested in glands and reflexes than in the autonomy of the spirit. Biological chemistry has weakened confidence in the worth of the human personality which a belief in immortality implies. The statistical study of social groups and the attempt to legislate men out of their vices have been expressions of a sense of impotence of the individual in the midst of social forces.

Over against all this is the conception of Jesus as to the place of goodwill and loving purpose in human life. There is no compromise between his view of the world and the mechanistic or deterministic. With him there is freedom and hope for men however socially submerged or economically dependent. They, too, may share in spiritual goods.

Chief among the basic desires of men Jesus would class the desire to know God, to know him not merely as a truth or principle, but personally. The cry of Philip, "Show us the Father," [1] was the outburst of humanity's heart, and the answer it drew forth has satisfied generations. And although Jesus does not describe with any detail the nature of this want of a more perfect knowledge of God, and treats it more as a need than as a desire, it is always present as a postulate controlling his preaching and life.[2] He had come that men might receive the divine life abundantly.

Whenever men grow confused about God and shrink from considering him personally they part with Jesus. The God he sets forth is not a personification of social values, an impersonal force, a half-distrusted response

[1] Luke 12:15.

[2] John 16:8-10. In this connection one recalls the eagerness with which Jesus is said to have met an honest seeker after truth like Nathaniel and Thomas, Zacchæus and Martha, as well as the earnestness, not to say severity, with which he answered those whose ignorance was in part due to their own failure to follow their better instincts, as Nicodemus and Philip. Compare also the philosophy by which the Fourth Gospel accounts for the presence or absence of the faith that accepts Jesus, John 3:18-21.

from forces upon which men feel themselves dependent in their search for something they desire. Jesus was no more a theological humanist than he was a philosophical determinist. He believes in a Father who cares for nature and human needs and social institutions. He can bring to pass results beyond the power of men. To him men may confidently pray, and for his establishment of a kingdom in which goodwill shall be supreme they may hopefully wait. If such a religious faith seems naïve to the sophisticated, he would have no quarrel with Jesus, for Jesus said that a man had to take the attitude of a child to appreciate the good news of a spiritual order and a loving God which he announced. Every follower of his must be possessed of the revolutionary and adventurous rather than the scientific psychology.

II

Jesus' teaching leads to a unification of the personality in social relations. It seems clear from a study of many instances that moral habits gained in one sphere of conduct do not always carry over into another. A man, for instance, will be honest in his business and be ready to cheat the railroad company out of his fare. Indeed, it has become a moot question whether disciplines can be transferred and there is any such thing as habit as distinct from habits. It is precisely upon this that Jesus insists. To him life is not atomistic. Habits are to be genetically the outcome of a dominant attitude. Could anything be plainer than in the instance of the rich young man who had all sorts of good habits but who lacked a unifying attitude? The difference between such a view and that of the behaviorist is clear enough. Its importance in the development of a social ethics is equally clear. A person dominated by the faith and hope of Jesus has been reborn into spiritual unity. Dissociated motives and localized habits have been replaced by a dominant attitude or mind-set toward the ideal of a social good. The significant fact, however, is that this ideal of Jesus is not abstract but concrete. Its morality furnishes a basis for education in actual conduct. Jesus thus makes prominent social rather than metaphysical goals. Neither the state nor society, abstract goodness nor duty, but a more personal because a more social individual, is the end of the quest for perfection. His teaching as to love, expressed in other words, means that social relations are functional, serving the progress of spiritual and personal values of the individual.

For Jesus trusted the inherent powers and capacities of the race. The ideal he portrayed was not intended for creatures less or more human than the restless men with whom he associated and out of whom he formed his following. Individual and social regeneration is possible because man and society are inherently salvable. And deep in the heart of a humanity that could be saved were its wants. Not that Jesus ever formally classifies them. Indeed he can hardly be said to recognize all their categories. But nevertheless he presupposes them. In his estimation they are in themselves morally neutral, yet according to the relative importance assigned to each of them they may express either a healthy or decadent personality. It is in this perspective in which he sees the various wants of men that Jesus shows the instinct of the practical man and not that of the fanatic. Thus in the case of purely physical wants, with a characteristic loyalty to his anti-ascetic ideals, Jesus assumes the legitimacy of the child's cry for food,[3] bids his disciples pray for bread,[4] and pities a multitude which he saw grow faint with hunger.[5] Yet physical wants are inferior to many others. Man is not to live by bread alone,[6] and spiritual intensity might altogether lift one, as it did himself, quite above mere physical hunger.[7] One of the sharpest rebukes he ever administered to his disciples was occasioned by their crass misinterpretation of one of his sayings as a caution against certain classes of bakers from whom they might be tempted to buy bread.[8] The same is true of all economic wants. Who better than Jesus ever appreciated the power of a merchant's desire to succeed in business,[9] or of a laborer's passion for a larger wage?[10] The Heavenly Father knows his children have need of food and raiment,[11] but just for that very reason men are not to make the search for them the chief end in life. A man's life does not consist in the abundance of things that he possesses.

The satisfaction, not of these lower wants, but of those other and higher desires for the more personal experiences of life, is in the new order of life. Men are not to be compelled to be good, but their desires are to lead them to goodness, or, if the desire be lacking, are to be convinced of the sin of the lack. Not obedience, but loving impulse, is the key to a unified character.

[3] Matt. 7:9.
[4] Matt. 6:11.
[5] Matt. 15:32; Mark 8:3.
[6] Matt. 4:4.
[7] Jn. 4:31-34.

[8] Matt. 16:5-12; Mk. 8:14-21.
[9] Matt. 13:45.
[10] Matt. 20:2sq.
[11] Matt. 6:31, 32; Jn. 6:27.

III

In the third place, Jesus teaches that goodwill is a practicable basis upon which to build human society. If individuals suffer in the attempt to live in accordance with such a conviction, it is either because they are indifferent to group solidarity or they are victims of those who prefer rights to giving justice. It would seem that such a major premise for organizing life and building social institutions would be accepted by those who have seen in him the incarnation of the Son of God, of the same substance as the Father, very God of very God, begotten, not made. But a theology has to be touched with social passion if it is to become a basis controlling social action. Most of us are too much like Peter, who in one breath declared his belief that Jesus was the Christ and in the next breath told him that his views were false. Nor can it be denied that it sometimes is difficult to admit that the maintenance of prejudice and privilege is not righteous. But it is one thing to be just and another thing to be fraternal and forgiving. If one does not believe that Jesus actually is setting forth a sane and healthy social principle, his Christology will be no more potent in social reorganization to-day than it was in the fifth century, when devotion to the Nicene Creed did not prevent the collapse of a civilization. Jesus was right when he insisted that unless one really believed that he was telling truth and organized life in accordance with his teachings, one would be as unstable as a house built upon sand.

Undeniably it is at this point that the real test faces modern men. Do they really believe that it is possible to organize society on the principles of Jesus?

Do they actually believe that acquisitiveness and hatred, the struggle to preserve rights, the refusal to democratize privilege are unsafe bases upon which to found society? Ten thousand years of human history ought to have made this plain, but the world still stands hesitant before treating the ideal of Jesus seriously. But no amount of respectability or orthodoxy or piety can be a substitute for such an attitude in our day any more than in the days of the Pharisees.

At all events, whether men dare accept it or not, whether the church makes it central or not, whether it seem true or not, Jesus taught that love is a practicable basis upon which to build human relations. Once let humanity actually believe this and the perspective of values will be changed. Giving justice will replace fighting for rights; the democratizing of privilege will replace the manipulation of social advantages; the humanizing of necessary economic processes will replace the exploiting of human life in the interests of wealth or pleasure.

It is a lordly act when for the good of the smaller and greater communities in which one lives this confidence in the teaching of Jesus is made supreme. Such followers of Jesus as make this decision may differ as to methods, but they can have no question as to principle; they may balance the call to martyrdom by the call to self-sacrificing moral education, but they will not deny their Master; they may differ as to theologies and ecclesiastical rites, but they will have one faith in the trustworthiness of the Founder of the movement to which they belong. Within that movement there will be education, art, philosophy, and scientific research; there will be social institutions and

ambitious altruism; but these all will be controlled
by that central attitude which Jesus described and so
uncompromisingly embodied. His followers will possess the zest of the revolutionist, the painstaking
method of the technician, the goodwill of the Heavenly
Father. But the greatest of these will be goodwill.

SUPPLEMENTARY NOTES
TO THE TEXT

Page

12 * Notice the way Mathews carefully applies his method to the problem of Jesus and his cultural milieu.

18 * C. C. McCown, himself a graduate of Chicago, developed this motif in his *The Genesis of the Social Gospel* (New York: Alfred A. Knopf, 1929).

20 * The socio-economic differences between Pharisees and Sadducees has been explored by Louis Finkelstein, *The Pharisees* (Philadelphia: Jewish Publication Society of America, 1938), vol. 1. Finkelstein argued that the struggle between the Pharisees and Sadducees reflected the original urban background of the former and the rural aristocracy of the latter. In the most recent edition (1962), he expressed himself somewhat more reservedly.

21 * Mathews's view of the Pharisees differs from that put forward by Jewish scholars. See, e.g., Louis Ginzberg, *Students, Scholars, and Saints* (Philadelphia: Jewish Publication Society of America, 1958).

22 * Mathews's view of continual agitations for insurrection against Rome has received independent support from William Farmer, *Maccabees, Zealots, and Josephus* (New York: Columbia University Press, 1956). The resistance movement against Rome prior

Page

to 70 c. e. has been investigated recently by Martin
Hengel, *Die Zeloten,* Arbeiten zur Geschichte des
Spätjudentums und Unchristentums 1. (Leiden : Brill,
1961).

27   * With the discovery of the so-called Dead Sea Scrolls
the picture of apocalyptic is even more complex.
Mathews's view of the mixture of military and theological perspectives has been supported by the War
Scroll which uses military know-how of the day to
speak of the final battle between the Sons of Light
and the Sons of Darkness. The definitive work on
this text was published by Yigael Yadin, *The War of
the Sons of Light Against the Sons of Darkness* (New
York: Oxford University Press, 1962).

30   * Mathews here refers to John 1:19–28, which most
scholars today are not prepared to take at face value
as Mathews apparently did. In *The Social Teachings
of Jesus* the same uncritical blending of John and the
synoptics appears. Cf. e.g., pp. 30 f., 71.

30   † Reimarus also emphasized the insurrectionist motif
in popular expectation, but argued that both Jesus
and John appropriated it uncritically—that is, both
were revolutionary agitators. See H. S. Reimarus,
Reimarus: Fragments in this series, ed. Charles Tal-
bert. S. G. F. Brandon, *Jesus and the Zealots* (New
York: Scribner's, 1968) has reopened the question,
but is more cautious in his reconstruction.

31   * The question of "the messianic self-consciousness
of Jesus" is a complex one that has been subject to
endless debate. In the present book Mathews assumes
that Jesus thought of himself as the Messiah, although
he does not spell out the details as he did, for example, in *The Messianic Hope in the New Testament,*
part 2. The question is still unsettled, and the literature is endless. For a recent statement denying that
Jesus used messianic categories in referring to him-

Page

self, see Günther Bornkamm, *Jesus of Nazareth*, trans. Irene and Fraser McLuskey (New York: Harper, 1960), pp. 169–178.

31 † Mathews here reflects the widespread view of the liberal Lives of Jesus, according to which the baptism story (Mk 1:9–11) reveals the inner experience of Jesus in which his "filial consciousness" emerged. Today, most critics refuse to use the story in this way, though affirming the fact that Jesus was baptized by John.

33 * Recently, this view has been questioned by Walter Wink, *John the Baptist in the Gospel Tradition*, Society for New Testament Studies Monograph Series 7 (New York: Cambridge University Press, 1968).

33 † Mathews alludes to the story in Lk 4:16–30. For a recent discussion of this story, see Hugh Anderson, "Broadening Horizons. The Rejection at Nazareth Pericope of Lk 4:16–30 in Light of Recent Critical Trends," *Interpretation* 18 (1964): 259–75.

34 * Here Mathews assumes that one can to this degree at least give some chronological order to the words and deeds of Jesus. Since the publication of Karl Ludwig Schmidt's *Der Rahmen der Geschichte Jesu* (1919), many scholars, particularly in Germany, have given up the attempt to date the events described in the Gospels in relationship to each other. On a good many issues Mathews is, of course, more confident regarding the results of a search for the Jesus of history than much Continental scholarship has been during most of the twentieth century. The story of the quest, its rejection, and its renewal is told briefly in Reginald H. Fuller, *The New Testament in Current Study* (New York: Scribner's, 1962), pp. 25–53, as well as in James M. Robinson's *A New Quest of the Historical Jesus* (London: SCM, 1961).

35 * The reference to Mk 10:62 is obviously wrong, since there is no such verse. Perhaps he means Lk 9:27.

Page

36   * During this period there was a good deal of discussion of the psychic soundness of Jesus, much of it having to do with the implications of his apocalyptic ideas and his consciousness of messianic eminence. The discussion is reviewed in Albert Schweitzer, *Die psychiatrische Beurteilung Jesu* (1913), English translation, *The Psychiatric Study of Jesus* (Boston: Beacon Press, 1948), and Walter E. Bundy, *The Psychic Health of Jesus* (London: Macmillan, 1922). The impetus of the psychiatric approach was considerably lessened by the influence of the sociological approach taken by Shirley Jackson Case in *Jesus: A New Biography* (Chicago: University of Chicago Press, 1927). Case's book, introduced by Robert W. Funk, is included in this series.

40   * Oscar Cullmann has also called attention to the presence of Zealots in the circle of Jesus' disciples in *The State in the New Testament* (New York: Scribner's, 1956) chap. 1. See also S. G. F. Brandon, *Jesus and the Zealots* (New York: Scribner's, 1968), chap. 7.

43   * Mathews seems to be debating with himself in the first three paragraphs of this chapter, and the result is rather cloudy. Admitting that the church may have modified the teachings of Jesus in the process of transmitting his sayings, he nevertheless is confident that the socio-historical method can pretty well decide what genuinely comes from Jesus. But then he points to the limits to which a modern historian can decide what ''a great soul'' may or may not have said. How can we be sure, then, that we have Jesus' thoughts but not necessarily his words? While he makes no reference here to the work of the Continental form-critics, he may have had in his mind some of the problems raised by them with regard to the problem of distinguishing between the original teachings of Jesus and their subsequent modification in

Page

order to meet the kerygmatic and didactic needs of the developing church.

44 * It is doubtful if any sociologist today would advance so simplistic an understanding of social institutions. For Mathews, of course, tracing institutions to attitudes was a convenient way of making Jesus germane to the social process.

45 * The reference to two strata here is puzzling. By what criteria does he make the distinctions he proceeds to relate? Mathews apparently relies on Mk 4 :10–12 and takes it to be an authentic saying of Jesus. Today it appears strange that Mathews, writing a generation after Wrede exposed the role of the "messianic secret" motif in Mark and interpreted this passage accordingly as Mark's own theology, would continue to use this text uncritically. Jeremias has tried to salvage the authenticity of the text by appealing to Greek mistranslation of the original Aramaic; but even if this were the case, Mark himself still understood the Greek wording to mean exactly what it says —that Jesus spoke in parables lest he be understood. Mathews makes the text mean that Jesus used parables lest he be *mis*understood. For Jeremias' view, see *The Parables of Jesus*, trans. S. H. Hooke from 6th Germ. ed. (New York: Scribner's, 1963) pp. 13–18.

48 * Mathews evidently trusted the narrative settings for the words of Jesus. Here is one of the points at which form criticism had a significant impact, for it showed that such settings are stylized and stem either from the Evangelists or their traditions, but cannot be presumed to be accurate reports of the original setting. Interestingly, Mathews nowhere refers to form critical work in this book, written nine years after K. L. Schmidt's *Der Rahmen der Geschichte Jesu* and seven years after the analyses of Martin Dibelius and Rudolf Bultmann. Recently, however,

Page

Mathews's trust in the narrative setting has been supported from an entirely different direction, "audience criticism" as developed by J. Arthur Baird, *Audience Criticism and the Historical Jesus* (Philadelphia: Westminster, 1969). Baird argues that "logion and audience were inseparable. Jesus was a selective teacher whose crisis message was. a net sifting one audience from another" (p. 137). This is doubtless a minority report today.

51   * It is significant that Mathews knows what Mt 5:48 means without examining linguistic evidence—that is, without asking for the presumed Aramaic Jesus might have used.

54   * Mathews's reliance on the conceptuality of moral idealism in order to organize and interpret the variegated teachings of Jesus is clear. In contrast with liberal theology in general, recent study of Jesus refuses to say that Jesus was concerned primarily with attitudes; instead, it is frequently pointed out that Jesus actually "radicalizes" the law and does not relativize it by concentrating on attitudes. See, e.g., Rudolf Bultmann, *Jesus and the Word* (New York: Scribner's, 1934 [paperback 1958]; 1st Germ. ed. 1926) pp. 72–86; 91 f., and Günther Bornkamm, *Jesus of Nazareth*, chap. 5. Even when Mathews sees the rigor of Jesus' teaching about divorce, he speaks in terms of ideals, not the law (cf. pp. 80–84; 125).

55   * Here we see Mathews's reliance on science to validate the permanent truth of Jesus' teaching (thereby separating it from the psychology of revolution!); see also the Introduction, pp. xxix–xxxi.

60   * For Mathews's concern with democratic ideals instead of monarchic ones, see Introduction, pp. xxviii–xxix. In this paragraph, Mathews apparently grounds his term "spiritual democracy" in the statement that "Jesus unqualifiedly condemned any limitation to the humblest soul's enjoyment of the forgiving love of God."

Page

60 † Since Mathews insists that he is working exegetically (see his note 31 on p. 61), one must conclude
that this sentence is his interpretation of Jesus' call
to repentance.

62 * This is an important paragraph for understanding
Mathews's views on the relationship of ethics and
eschatology. The reference to "interim *mores*" has
in mind the thesis of Albert Schweitzer that the ethics
of Jesus apply only to the interim between the
announcement of the kingdom and its arrival.
Mathews argues instead that while many of the specific details of Jesus' teachings are relative to the
society of his day, the fundamental demand that men
show goodwill to each other is a timeless moral absolute relevant to all situations. The attempt to demonstrate that the essential foundation of the ethical
imperatives of Jesus is the character and will of God
and that they are therefore valid independently of
their apocalyptic setting is widespread. Cf., for example, the treatment of these issues in Amos Wilder,
Ethics and Eschatology in the Teachings of Jesus
(New York: Harper, 1939), especially pp. 125–166,
and in Paul Ramsey, *Basic Christian Ethics* (New
York: Scribner's, 1951), pp. 24–45.

65 * Here Mathews anticipates one line of interpretation
given special prominence in the "new quest" of the
historical Jesus, especially in the work of Ernst
Fuchs. See E. Fuchs, *Studies of the Historical Jesus*,
trans. Andrew Scobie, Studies in Biblical Theology 42
(Naperville: Allenson, 1964; Germ. ed. 1960). ". . .
what Jesus, in fact, demands of his hearers is a
decision. . . . Thus the central theme of the sayings of
Jesus is the decision which they demand. But this
demand is simply the echo of Jesus' own decision. We
have to understand his conduct as likewise determined
by a decision, and we can infer what he did from
what he demanded" (p. 22 f.). "To have faith in
Jesus now means essentially to repeat Jesus' decision" (p. 28). See also p. 30. Faith as "repeating

Page

the decision of Jesus'' is reflected also in Fuchs's discussion of prayer. See the essay ''Jesus and Faith'' in
the aforementioned volume, p. 63 f. (see also pp. 100–
103; 184 f.; 222–28).

122   * Mathews's view of earliest Christianity as unstruc-
tured and nontheological has not been vindicated.
One surmises that it is Mathews the liberal theologian,
not Mathews the sociologist, who speaks here.

123   * The text is confused, because the typesetter mis-
placed an entire line. The sentence should omit the
third line from the bottom of the paragraph so as to
read, ''The growing identification of ecclesiastical
with political interests, all tended'' etc. This line
should have been the second line of type in the new
section, so as to read, ''Sooner or later goodwill
becomes a problem of social technique, and such technique is a matter of science rather than of motive.''
Restoring the single line in this way avoids nonsense
in both places.

127   * Here Mathews the historian of Jesus comes to terms
with Mathews the modernist theologian. In this way
he cuts the ground from under a biblicistic appeal to
Jesus; doubtless the fundamentalistic opposition to
the Social Gospel is in the background.

133   * Were Mathews not a modernist but a traditional
theologian he would have spoken of the relation
between man and God. This page ought to suffice to
show that the ''Fathers'' of the Social Gospel were
far more deeply rooted in the Christian tradition than
'they are sometimes credited with having been, or than
some of their offspring were later.

145   * It should not be overlooked that Mathews turned
this chapter, which was not present in *The Social
Teachings of Jesus*, into an apology for the Social
Gospel in light of his understanding of Jesus. In
making this move, he ignored themes commonly found
in such a chapter: resurrection and the rise of the
church, or sacraments.

INDEX